HAUNTED HOTELS of SOUTHERN COLORADO

HAUNTED HOTELS OF SOUTHERN COLORADO

NANCY WILLIAMS

Published by Haunted America
A Division of The History Press
Charleston, SC
www.historypress.com

Copyright © 2019 by Nancy K. Williams
All rights reserved

Front cover: Cliff House, Colorado Springs. *Courtesy of Tom Williams.*
Back cover, top: Victor Hotel, Victor; *bottom*: Imperial Hotel, Cripple Creek.
Both courtesy of Tom Williams.

First published 2019

Manufactured in the United States

ISBN 9781467141970

Library of Congress Control Number: 2019943364

Notice: The information in this book is true and complete to the best of our knowledge. It is offered without guarantee on the part of the author or The History Press. The author and The History Press disclaim all liability in connection with the use of this book.

All rights reserved. No part of this book may be reproduced or transmitted in any form whatsoever without prior written permission from the publisher except in the case of brief quotations embodied in critical articles and reviews.

*This book is dedicated to
Wendy Williams for shared laughter and the fun of being on the road again.
Tom Williams for guiding me to the tops of high peaks and beautiful
mountains—to abandoned mines and forgotten towns.*

CONTENTS

Acknowledgements	9
Introduction	11
1. Colorado Springs	15
2. Manitou Springs	22
3. Trinidad	29
4. Del Norte	36
5. South Fork	43
6. Creede	49
7. Antonito	55
8. Durango	60
9. Silverton	73
10. Ouray	90
11. Telluride	112
12. Dolores	123
13. Delta	129
14. Grand Junction	138
15. Paonia	146
16. Crested Butte	153
17. Cripple Creek	162
18. Victor	175
Bibliography	185
About the Author	189

Acknowledgements

A special thank-you to Wendy Williams, whose photographs captured the charm and unique aspects of these historic landmarks.

Thank you to Tom Williams, whose expertise with the camera always results in a perfect photograph.

A thank-you to the local librarians and the regional historical societies who have answered questions and guided me through their special collections.

My thanks to all who shared their stories and experiences, adding so much authenticity to this book.

Thank you to all the hotel and inn owners who allowed me to explore their basements and attics.

Thanks and much appreciation to Artie Crisp, senior acquisitions editor, The History Press.

Introduction

General William Palmer, a retired Civil War general, dreamed of building a railroad south from Denver to Mexico City. His experience on the plains and in the mountains laying the Union Pacific tracks westward to complete the nation's first transcontinental railroad convinced him of the potential of the Rocky Mountain West. He was enthusiastic about the opportunities presented by its vast open lands, mild climate, and grasslands with their agricultural possibilities.

The West was separated from the rest of the country by distance and semiarid regions, but Palmer believed it could develop a self-sufficient, independent economy by raising its own crops and livestock, mining its own coal and minerals, and developing productive industries.

Palmer believed the Rocky Mountain West needed a regional railroad system to pull it together and unite its integral parts. He envisioned a railroad that ran from north to south, with connecting lines to settlements in valleys and up the canyons to mining camps. To achieve this, in 1870, Palmer organized the Denver & Rio Grande Railroad. This would be a narrow-gauge railroad whose smaller engines could maneuver more easily around the sharp curves and handle the steep mountain grades. He planned the first section and began laying tracks south from Denver to Santa Fe. By 1871, the Denver & Rio Grande Railroad had reached the base of Pike's Peak, where Palmer planned the city of Colorado Springs.

Work stopped for four years while Palmer raised money to lay tracks south to Trinidad and Raton Pass. This delay cost the D&RG its monopoly on

Introduction

Southern Colorado. The Atchison, Topeka, and Santa Fe Railroad, which was laying its tracks west from Kansas, reached Raton Pass one day ahead of Palmer. A contract was made that gave the rival railroad the right of way over the pass into New Mexico. Palmer could no longer continue south, so he turned the railroad toward the west.

By 1878, the D&RG tracks were snaking their way across the San Luis Valley toward the silver camps of the San Juan Mountains. The towns of Colorado Springs, Manitou Springs, Alamosa, and Antonito had been founded by Palmer, and his land companies were promoting them. The railroad boosted industrial and commercial growth and provided a means of getting agricultural products to market. Palmer placed advertisements in the United States and Great Britain promoting the agricultural and the commercial opportunities presented by ownership of parcels of land near the railroad. These new towns were ideal locations for supply centers, mills, and smelters, and the railroad would get agricultural, industrial, and commercial products to market.

The fabulously rich discoveries of silver and gold in the San Juan Mountains had not been developed because their remote locations made transportation very expensive. All supplies, food, and equipment had to be hauled in by pack trains, which also carried the rich ore to smelters for processing. The eastern newspapers described the San Juan Mountains as "the wealthiest district in the wide west," but this did not bring wealthy investors. Production and transportation costs were higher than the profits. It was obvious that reliable transportation was vital to the development of the mines in the San Juan Mountains.

The arrival of the Denver & Rio Grande Railroad lowered the costs of mining and attracted investors. This money went into developing rich strikes and supported more mineral discoveries. Silver and gold ore from the mines in the mountains were shipped by rail to the smelters at Denver and Pueblo. The value of the precious metals remained the same, but every factor of their production went down. The cost of machinery was less, and the price of food, clothing, and fuel dropped, while mills and smelters operated more cheaply.

Historian Herbert Brayer wrote, "It was essentially the railroad and in an equal measure the land companies it founded that gave substance to the development of south and west Colorado." The Denver & Rio Grande was responsible for the development and expansion of the mining industry and the tremendous growth and development of Southern Colorado. Alamosa, Colorado Springs, Antonito, and Durango were founded by the Denver

Introduction

& Rio Grande Railroad. Commerce generated by the railroad supported business and economic growth, and the population of this part of the state increased dramatically.

The Silver Decade, a period of spectacular expansion from the 1880s through 1892, was an exciting time of immense wealth in Colorado. Ramshackle mining camps grew into bustling cities, and poor prospectors became overnight millionaires. Luxurious hotels and modest boardinghouses were built in towns that flourished in the railroad's shadow. Many of these historic buildings were lost to neglect and deterioration, consumed by fires or demolished in the name of progress. A few were rescued by local citizens, who recognized the importance of preserving these historic landmarks. They were restored with historic grants, donations, community fundraisers, and innovative programs. Today, these hotels are listed in the National Register of Historic Places, included in a National Historic District, are Landmark Hotels, or have been designated a local historical landmark. They are full of memories of the past and a few spirits, too. Ghosts of yesterday still roam the halls and whisper on the stairs. Their footsteps are heard in the night, and their shadows may drift through your dreams.

1
COLORADO SPRINGS

General Palmer began laying tracks for his narrow-gauge railroad, the Denver & Rio Grande, heading south from Denver. Once the high plain near the base of Pike's Peak was reached, Palmer formed a land company and platted his dream city. He envisioned a utopian community without the usual problems of crime, congestion, smoke, and noise that confronted most cities. Its residents would live free of class strife and difficult social problems. The new city, originally called the "Fountain Colony," would cover seventy blocks of broad, tree-shaded avenues, with numerous parks and free lots set aside for churches and schools.

Colorful advertisements were placed in newspapers in the eastern United States and Great Britain describing the climate and attractions of the area. It was soon obvious that this would become a community for the wealthy. Membership was open to anyone who was a teetotaler, had good moral character, and could afford a $100 land certificate, plus the additional purchase price of a lot, a house, and any other permanent buildings, like a carriage house. Palmer wanted this community to become "the most attractive place for homes in the West" and welcomed first-class newspapers, schools, and colleges.

The response to Palmer's advertisements was overwhelming, and in less than a year, the Fountain Colony's Town Company had been inundated with inquiries. Thousands of possible residents toured the area and sampled the nearby mineral springs. Friends persuaded Palmer to change the name of the planned community to "Colorado Springs," which resonated with buyers. They rushed to purchase lots and were soon building Tudor-style homes and massive stone churches, lining the main street, Cascade Avenue, with impressive brick commercial buildings.

Some scions of eastern high society who came to Colorado Springs were fascinated by the British and their customs. The Brits, with their stylish fashions, snooty chefs, and pink-cheeked governesses, intrigued them. Local gentlemen adopted knickerbockers and plaid stockings for their rugby and cricket games. They took up polo and donned bright red jackets to "ride to the hounds," chasing foxes through the huge rock monoliths of Garden of the Gods. Of course, if a fox wasn't handy, a wily coyote would do. After these hunts, despite Palmer's teetotaling plans for Colorado Springs, the hunters celebrated a successful day with drinks at the new Cheyenne Mountain Country Club. White ties and tails were mandatory, even at informal dinners, where the fancy menus included mutton, roast beef or broilers dressed up in paper pantalettes. Jackrabbit was carefully prepared, following the recipe for English hare from *Warne's English Cookbook*. The town vibrated with clipped Harvard, Oxford, and Main Line Back Bay Boston accents, and although christened Colorado Springs, it was soon nicknamed "Little London."

During the 1870s, many finely bred, well-accented young Englishmen were drawn to this area, eager to acquire a piece of land in the American West. Some purchased large parcels and started huge cattle ranches and livestock-related businesses. Others began commercial enterprises, like the ironworks that produced ornamental ironwork and structural iron used in construction and roofs. There was even a demand for fine wire fencing used to surround the new Tudor mansions. Quarries produced tons of high-quality limestone and sandstone used in buildings throughout the state.

James Hagerman, an ambitious Canadian, had amassed a large fortune in the steel business, but in the process, he acquired consumption (tuberculosis). He'd come to Colorado Springs in 1884, an emaciated invalid, expected to die within a few weeks. He surprised himself, his family and friends, and his business associates by improving enough to develop a plan to build a standard-gauge railroad. It would rival General Palmer's smaller narrow-gauge railroad, the Denver & Rio Grande, which was busily laying its tracks south toward Pueblo and Trinidad.

Hagerman planned to take his new Colorado Midland Railroad west over the Continental Divide to Leadville and Aspen. He hoped to obtain lucrative contracts to haul silver ore from the booming mines to smelters and, in turn, to return with coal, goods, and equipment for the mines and the bustling towns. Hagerman's partners included Aspen developer Jerome Wheeler, who helped raise $7 million for the project. Unfortunately, they underestimated the difficulties of constructing a railroad over the Continental Divide. Workers struggled to build a roadbed and then lay the tracks up steep mountain grades, often through deep snow drifts. They were battered by blizzards and frigid winter storms, which halted work. Since they could not build over every high-altitude summit, they had to blast eight tunnels through the Rocky Mountains. Then they built countless bridges across raging rivers and yawning chasms and made endless detours around obstacles. Hagerman's expensive, foolhardy project was finally completed, and the first engine of the Colorado Midland Railroad chugged into Aspen in 1888. It arrived months behind the Denver & Rio Grande and lost the lucrative contracts to haul silver ore.

While Hagerman struggled to dynamite passages through mountains, plans were underway to build a cog railroad to the top of Pike's Peak. The Manitou and Pike's Peak Cog Railway Company was formed by Zalman Simmons, who'd founded the Simmons Beautyrest Mattress Company. When construction began in 1889, a two-day mule trip or a vigorous hike could get a visitor to the summit. Work was also done on a rough carriage road, and by 1893, Katherine Bates made the bumpy buggy trip to the top of Pike's Peak. Bates was an English professor who'd come west to teach at the new Colorado College in Colorado Springs. The breathtaking view inspired Bates to write a poem, which, when set to music, became the well-loved patriotic song "America the Beautiful."

When the Pike's Peak Cog Railroad was completed, its first passenger train carried an entire church choir to the summit on June 30, 1891. Colorado Springs was attracting thousands of visitors; they were enchanted by the scenery, the grandeur of the Rockies, and the romance of the West. They basked in the sunshine and enjoyed the balmy climate, which bolstered its reputation as a health resort. Americans, especially those suffering from tuberculosis and respiratory diseases, flocked to Colorado, fleeing the cold, damp East. During the 1870s and 1880s, it was estimated that over one third of the state's population was composed of recovering invalids.

The discovery of gold in Cripple Creek brought money pouring into Colorado Springs, and fifty overnight millionaires built their mansions along Wood Avenue. The offices of more than 420 mining companies lined Tejon Avenue, and the town's population soared to thirty-five thousand. By 1894, there were three stock exchanges trading more shares than any other exchange in the world.

Spencer Penrose and several other friends from wealthy backgrounds headed for Cripple Creek, where they became involved in various aspects of mining and associated industries. They labored mightily at their jobs in the mines and hot mills and drove stages and freight wagons during the day. At night, they were transformed into gay blades in white ties and tails who cruised down the mountain to squire pretty Colorado Springs girls to dinner dances at the sophisticated Antlers Hotel. Bert Carlton, who came west a tubercular but defeated the disease, drove a Colorado Springs horse car. Then he clerked in a store until he had enough money to buy a freight wagon, which he used to haul coal to the mines and return with a load of ore. He often took stock in gold mines as payment for his freighting services, and before long, he owned several gold mines.

Spencer Penrose became a venture capitalist and made a fortune in Cripple Creek. He used his vast resources to build a highway to the top of Pike's Peak, established the Cheyenne Mountain Zoo, and financed the elegant Broadmoor Hotel. He acquired the Pike's Peak Cog Railway in 1925, and he and his wife, Julie, established the El Pomar Foundation to support Colorado nonprofit organizations involved in health, human services, education, arts and humanities, and civic and community initiatives. Today, the El Pomar Foundation's assets total more than $500 million. It contributes over $20 million annually through grants and community stewardship programs.

Colorado Springs developed a strong military presence when Camp Carson was opened in the 1940s. Construction was started on the Air Force Academy in 1954, and today the area is home to Fort Carson, Peterson Air Force Base, the U.S. Space Command NORAD (North American Aerospace Defense Command), and Schriever Air Force Base.

Colorado Springs has always attracted visitors, from the earliest time when ancient people gathered at the nearby mineral springs. Today, over five million people visit this popular Rocky Mountain city annually.

Broadmoor Hotel

The Broadmoor, a tall, pink-stucco, Italian Renaissance–style hotel, looms over colorful flowers, manicured lawns and lush grounds. A large marble fountain splashes water into a lily pond in front of the porte-cochere. The Broadmoor is a member of the Historic Hotels of America, and it is a Forbes Five-Star and AAA Five-Diamond luxury resort.

The hotel sits at the base of Cheyenne Mountain where a herd of dairy cows once grazed. Those cows belonged to a German immigrant, Count James Pourtales, who'd come to America in 1884 with hopes of rebuilding his family's fortune. He bought the small Broadmoor Dairy Farm outside Colorado Springs, acquired more cows and purchased an additional 2,500 acres. Then he bought more land, divided it into residential lots, and built the Cheyenne Mountain Country Club. He added a golf course, tennis courts, and a polo field for members and their guests. In 1891, Pourtales built the Broadmoor Casino, which opened with fireworks, balloonists, and tight-rope walkers. Since the casino was outside Colorado Springs, which banned alcoholic beverages, it offered liquor and gambling and enjoyed a booming business.

During the depression of 1893, when people no longer had money to squander on gambling or liquor, the Count fell deeply into debt. In 1897, the casino burned to the ground, and although he eventually rebuilt, Pourtales never recouped his losses. He sold his Broadmoor properties to the estate of Winfield Scott, who'd died in 1902. Wealthy young Spencer Penrose, who had become a millionaire investing in Cripple Creek gold mines, bought the Broadmoor properties in 1916.

Penrose wanted to build a grand hotel, and in 1917, he had railroad tracks laid to it so concrete and steel could be brought in more easily. Work began on the hotel, and after completion of a nine-story tower, wings were added to each side. This gave the Italian Renaissance–style hotel 350 rooms with private baths. The spectacular hotel had sparkling crystal chandeliers, hand-painted ceilings and beams, imported wallpaper, and a curved marble staircase led upstairs from the spacious lobby. Guests enjoyed the luxurious accommodations and dined on sumptuous meals served in the elegant dining room. They played golf on the eighteen-hole course, fished in the well-stocked lake, and danced the night away in the huge ballroom.

The gala opening of the Broadmoor was the big event of the 1918 social season, and Penrose brought one hundred of his friends from New York in luxurious private railroad cars. A resourceful anti-prohibitionist, Penrose advised his guests to "bring five bottles of your favorite cologne, drinkable, of course!" The train brought four flat-bed cars loaded with "gasoline" and guarded by U.S. marshals. These railroad cars were hidden away in tunnels beneath the hotel.

Bottle Alley on the main floor is a collection of over ten thousand bottles of pre–World War I liquors from Spencer Penrose's private cellar. There are sealed bottles of some of the finest and rarest spirits ever produced, while

The Broadmoor was never dry during Prohibition. Its "Bottle Alley" contains a collection of Pre–World War I liquors from Spencer Penrose's private cellar. *Courtesy of Tom Williams.*

others have Penrose's notations about the occasions when their contents were enjoyed. The contents of two bottles were consumed when Julie and "Spec" Penrose traveled down the Nile, and one bottle was signed by George W. Bush when he celebrated his fortieth birthday at the hotel.

Fun-loving Spencer Penrose died in 1939, but his hotel continues to attract foreign dignitaries, statesmen, and celebrities. Nine presidents have laid their heads on the Broadmoor's downy pillows, and several kings, princes, and princesses with their large entourages, have swept through its stunning lobby. There are 779 rooms, eighteen restaurants and cafés, three golf courses, and a world-class spa.

Ghosts

It isn't surprising that some guests who once enjoyed the refined opulence of the "Grand Dame of the Rockies" have extended their stay for over one hundred years. There have been many sightings of ghosts and wispy apparitions by employees and guests.

The apparition of a pretty young woman, a flapper of the 1920s, has been seen around the hotel for years. Sometimes she's walking down the hall or waiting near the elevator, and then she vanishes. Hotel guests have complained about their television sets turning on and off by themselves. Personal items are moved about the room, and their alarm clocks go crazy. Employees and guests say they have heard mysterious voices, often on quiet stairs or in empty stairwells.

A team of paranormal investigators spent several days at the Broadmoor and obtained an interesting photo of a small, filmy figure before it disappeared. There's a labyrinth of tunnels running beneath the hotel which are used to move furniture, crates and boxes, and supplies from one building to another. Some areas are used only to store furniture. Spencer Penrose hid his flatbeds of liquor down here during Prohibition. Rumors have persisted for years that these tunnels under the hotel are haunted.

2
Manitou Springs

The picturesque box canyon at the base of Pike's Peak was a sacred spot for the Mountain Utes, who believed its bubbling springs cured the aches and pains of rheumatism and eased digestive troubles. The Arapaho and Cheyenne tribes often came to the springs before buffalo hunts, shared the healing gifts of the medicinal waters, and left offerings of beads and fetishes for the spirits. Archaeologists say ancient people gathered here as early as 1330 BC, and their grinding stones and artifacts, dating back over 3,500 years, have been found in nearby Garden of the Gods.

In 1820, Dr. Edwin James, the botanist with Stephen Long's expedition, discovered the mineral springs, and soon other early explorers were investigating the strange rumblings of gas born in deep aquifers escaping through the rocks. Others came to see if the cold, carbonated mineral waters really could soothe their upset stomachs and calm their anxieties. Explorer John Fremont camped near the springs when he was returning from California in 1844. In 1845, George Ruxton, a young English adventurer and military officer, praised the powers of the mineral springs in his bestselling book *Life in the Far West*. The springs became well known during the 1859 Pike's Peak Gold Rush, and prospectors often camped nearby.

General Palmer and his partner, Dr. William Bell, visited the mineral springs in 1868 and envisioned a first-class health resort and spa centered around them. Three years later, in 1871, while planning the route for their fledgling railroad, they designed a rail line from Colorado Springs to the site of their future resort.

Palmer raised money for railroad construction and to buy land. He designed another community, which he named "La Font." He thought this name added a touch of elegance and would attract wealthy residents and even more investors. There were over 400 large lots, suitable for plush villas, lining the resort's gracefully curving streets; 150 additional town lots were set aside for business locations and more modest residences. Charming pathways wound around the mineral springs, which were sheltered by rustic pagodas. Benches were placed strategically so visitors could "take the waters" while admiring the beauty of the area.

Palmer and Bell wrote advertisements touting the restorative powers of the soda springs and placed them in newspapers in the East and Great Britain. An Englishman, William Blackmore, was enthusiastic about Colorado's first resort and urged Palmer to change "La Font" to "Manitou." This was the Algonquin word for the "Great Spirit," and it was used in Longfellow's popular poem *The Song of Hiawatha*. Blackmore was fascinated by Indian lore, and when Palmer asked him to name the mineral springs, he continued the Native American theme.

General Palmer and Dr. Bell built a hotel they called the Manitou House for their first visitors. The celebrated arrivals included the Canon of Westminster, author Helen Hunt Jackson and Charles Kingsley, a priest of the Church of England, who was also a writer and social reformer. On opening day, August 13, 1872, forty-eight of the hotel's fifty-two rooms were occupied, and the Palmers, Bells, and their friends held a huge gala celebration.

Soon, sick but very wealthy visitors from the East were flocking to Manitou to "take the waters" to relieve their muscle and joint ailments and gastrointestinal distress. The mineral waters were also credited with curing tuberculosis, pneumonia, bronchitis, plus "derangement of the liver, spleen, and kidneys, nervous afflictions," as well as gout and alcoholism.

In 1880, the depot for the railroad line from Colorado Springs was completed, and former president General Ulysses S. Grant was a guest of honor at the gala celebration. The pink and white sandstone depot followed the plans originally designed to build a large church, the Manitou Springs Church of England. When completed, it was the only railroad depot in the country with a pulpit and stained-glass windows.

A large bathhouse and a bottling plant were built near the Navajo Spring, and by 1881, seven elegant resorts were offering first-class, plush accommodations. There were plenty of modest hotels, boardinghouses, and vacation cottages for visitors with smaller purses in the "Saratoga of

The Cliff House's original Rocky Mountain Victorian architecture of the late 1800s has been restored after a disastrous fire. *Courtesy of Tom Williams.*

the West." In 1890, millionaire Jerome Wheeler, who'd been instrumental in the economic development of Aspen, moved to Manitou Springs in hopes his wife's health would improve. He opened the Manitou Mineral Water Bottling Company in a three-story building near Navajo Spring and commemorated the occasion by donating a fine, four-sided clock to the city. Cast in Italy, the clock was also a fountain, where water flowed from dolphins' heads into bowls and additional basins around the base where man's best friend could drink. The elaborate clock-fountain was topped with a statue of Hebe, the goddess of health and healing. It can be seen in a park near the Cliff House Hotel.

The invention of the automobile brought more visitors to Manitou Springs, but these transient travelers spent less time at the grand hotels and more time exploring the area's attractions. By 1912, the resort town had a modern water system, electricity, telephones, and a trolley line to Colorado Springs. As the years passed, some of the mineral springs failed, while others were damaged by floods, but tourists continued to visit. Some decided to stay in Manitou Springs, doubling the 1950 population of about 2,500 people to 5,000 by 2013.

Many of the fine resort hotels were lost to deterioration and neglect, while others burned down or were converted into apartments. Since 1980, the Manitou Springs Historic District has managed all development, renovation, and preservation done within the city limits. The entire town is included in the National Register of Historic Places, making it one of the country's largest National Historic Districts. Now the mineral springs are protected by the Mineral Springs Foundation and can be enjoyed by locals and tourists.

CLIFF HOUSE

The elegant Cliff House, once known as the Inn, was built in 1873 on the route to South Park and Leadville to provide lodging to stagecoach passengers. By 1876, Manitou's springs of carbonated mineral water were drawing many visitors, and the Inn's twenty rooms were always full. Tents were put up outside to accommodate the overflow guests, who often gathered on the spacious veranda after dining at the inn.

During the 1870s, Edward Nichols came west to battle tuberculosis in Colorado's sunshine and dry climate. As his health improved, he bought a house and moved his wife and four children to Manitou Springs. Nichols became involved in community affairs, was elected mayor, and served eight terms.

In 1886, Nichols bought the Inn, renamed it the Cliff House, remodeled it and converted its twenty rooms into a luxurious four-story building. During this time, there was a lot of competition between hotel owners, eager to attract guests with their plush accommodations and by providing additional services. For example, when the Colorado Springs Hotel added ceiling fans in its dining room, "to keep the pesky flies off the dining tables," a rival built a bowling alley in his hotel. The Cliff House installed a cascading fountain in the flower garden.

In 1914, Edward Nichols and Colorado's Governor Shoup founded the Manitou Bath House Company and began promoting the healing properties of the numerous nearby springs. Nichols planned large formal dinners for the Cliff House guests that were followed by concerts on the hotel's lawn. Then before everyone retired for the night, it was customary for the guests to saunter over to the Bath House and Spa for glasses of fresh spring water. Meanwhile, bellboys went through the hotel carrying trays of sparkling mineral water for indisposed guests who couldn't walk to the spa.

Guests lounged on the Cliff House's veranda, watching the celebrities and gossiping about their peccadillos. Teddy Roosevelt stayed there twice, and Thomas Edison; Ferdinand, the crown prince of Austria; William Henry

The Cliff House, a stagecoach stop in 1874, became one of the first luxury health resorts in Manitou Springs. *Courtesy of History Colorado.*

Jackson, photographer of the West; showman P.T Barnum; Clark Gable; F.W. Woolworth of dime-store fame; and millionaire J. Paul Getty, all laid their heads on the Cliff House's fluffy pillows.

The good times at the Cliff House were swept away in 1921 by a disastrous flash flood. Walls of water roared down the canyon and swept through the hotel, wiping out the restaurant and soaking its floors. Completely submerged in water, the wooden planks warped and buckled so badly that they were pushed up to touch the ceiling. The Cliff House slowly recovered, but it never regained its past grandeur, and in 1981, it was purchased by a real estate developer, James Morley. He planned to remodel the hotel into a forty-two-unit apartment building, but before work began, there was a fire in March 1982. The roof was totally destroyed, and extensive water damage devastated the interior and threatened the entire building. Morley shelved his remodeling plans and let the damaged building sit vacant for the next sixteen years.

Since the Cliff House had been placed in the National Register of Historic Places in 1980, before the fire, any remodeling or renovations that were done had to restore the original Rocky Mountain Victorian architecture of the late 1800s. Modern amenities and current technology could be incorporated into the original design, but this would require at least $10.5 million. In September 2007, the hotel was sold to a Texas corporation, which spent $12 million restoring the hotel to its original Victorian style. An upscale dining room, including a large bar and grill, was added, and al fresco dining was available on the Veranda.

Ghosts

Many of Edward Nichols' employees remained at their posts for years, but one deserves a special longevity award for his service. Albert Whitehead worked at the hotel for fifteen years as a bellhop, and then he was promoted to night watchman. On the evening of July 11, 1913, guests relaxing on the veranda were horrified to see Albert, covered in blood, being chased by two masked thugs. They'd burst into his office demanding money and jewelry from the safe, and then without warning, they shot him. Albert collapsed on the lawn, and the thieves ran off into the night. The shocked guests rushed for a doctor, while others tried to help the wounded man. Despite the best medical care, Albert died two days later. He was laid to rest in the Crystal

Hills Cemetery, mourned by his wife and sons, fellow workers, and more than four hundred friends. The murderers were never caught.

On July 11, 1914, the first anniversary of the crime, the hotel's guests were enjoying a moonlight serenade when a lady suddenly jumped up shrieking. The others gasped when they saw a shadowy man stagger out the foyer doors and stumble off into the darkness, leaving a trail of bloody footprints. One of the guests, a physician, rushed after him, following the bloody trail until the footprints just disappeared into thin air. The frightened guests were interviewed by the police, but their investigation turned up nothing.

Through the years, a shadowy figure is occasionally seen running from the hotel into the night. This happened so many times that management called a psychic to learn more about this paranormal activity. The psychic conducted a séance, and although she did not know about the murder, she concluded that the spirit had once worked at the hotel. She said that he was unaware of his own tragic death. He was "stuck," unable to move on, doomed to wander for eternity. She explained that the frightening apparition was caused by residual energy as the spirit relived his own death over and over.

Today, some employees believe the faithful watchman is still keeping a protective eye on the Cliff House. When items disappear, doors open and close without visible human hand, or there are mysterious sounds, employees say "Just ask the ghost!" or "I don't know what happened—maybe the ghost does."

3
TRINIDAD

Trinidad sits on the banks of the Purgatory River in a pleasant, cottonwood-shaded valley. Old artifacts, petroglyphs, and adobe structures were left here through the centuries by many different peoples. The valley was home to prehistoric civilizations more than four hundred years before Columbus set foot on this continent. In 1593, the priest accompanying a Spanish expedition named the river that runs through it "Rio de las Animas Perdidas en Purgatorio." This translates to "The River of Lost Souls in Purgatory," and legend says the expedition priest named it in memory of a soldier who drowned in the river. When French trappers came looking for beaver in the 1700s, the Spanish name Purgatorio became the Purgatoire. By 1806, American mountain men venturing into the Rockies to trap beaver twisted the river's French name into the Picketwire or simply called it the Purgatory.

The Spanish government had forbidden trade with the French and Americans, so in 1821, when Mexico won its freedom from Spain, the door was thrown open to traders. Settlers in Santa Fe were eager for all kinds of goods, and William Becknell, a St. Louis trader, was the first to load a pack train with $3,000 worth of calico, cloth, beads, and goods and head west toward Santa Fe.

When Becknell reached the Purgatoire River, near the site of present-day Trinidad, he crossed rugged Raton Pass and went south to Santa Fe. The Spanish settlers were eager to trade, and Becknell quickly sold all of his goods and returned to Missouri with his pack mules loaded with bags of

Mexican pesos and bundles of furs. Becknell made an enormous profit, more than $90,000, and news of his success spread quickly. Soon traders with dollar signs in their eyes and loaded pack trains and wagons were headed for the markets in Taos and Santa Fe. They followed Becknell's route, which became known as the Mountain Branch of the Santa Fe Trail.

Weary traders and pioneers headed west welcomed the respite when they reached the Purgatoire River near present-day Trinidad. Everyone relaxed in the shade of a large grove of cottonwood trees, while their oxen and mules grazed on the thick grass. Animals and people needed to regain their strength before making the difficult crossing of Raton Pass. The treacherous trail over the pass was narrow, steep, and rocky. Often the wagons' wooden axles snapped, and their wheels were shredded by the brutally rough terrain.

In 1846, when the Mexican-American War erupted, General Stephen Kearney led the Army of the West of 1,600 volunteer troopers south across Raton Pass. Santa Fe was captured, and Mexico gave up Texas, California, most of Arizona, Nevada and Utah, part of Wyoming, much of Southern Colorado, and half of New Mexico in the Treaty of Guadalupe Hidalgo.

During the Civil War, the Mountain Route of the Santa Fe Trail was used by the Union army to move troops and supplies into the Southwest. Raton Pass was guarded by Union troops until the end of the Civil War. After 1865, the Raton Pass trail was blasted wider and graded into a usable toll road by retired mountain man and entrepreneur Uncle Dick Wooten. The rolling grasslands around Trinidad became a major sheep producer, and when the road over the pass was improved, travel became easier. Often up to five hundred head of wagon train oxen could be seen grazing on the lush riverside grass, preparing for the journey over Raton Pass. It usually took shepherds an entire day to get a large herd of ten thousand sheep safely across. Cattlemen Charles Goodnight and Oliver Loving paid Wooten ten cents a head to bring thousands of Texas longhorns over the pass on their way north to Denver.

In 1860, twelve families from Mora, New Mexico, led by Felipe and Delores Baca, settled in the fertile valley of the Purgatoire River. They named their settlement "Trinidad," derived from the Spanish for "Trinity." The new community became a supply center for neighboring farms and sheep and cattle ranches. By 1869, Trinidad's population had grown to 1,200, and log and adobe buildings lined Main and Commercial Streets. More Hispanic families came from New Mexico and settled west of Trinidad in the vast San Luis Valley.

During the late 1870s, the Denver & Rio Grande Railroad was in a race with the Atchison, Topeka, and Santa Fe to be the first to reach Trinidad. Both were anxious to make a deal with Uncle Dick Wooten for the right of way across Raton Pass, the only railroad route into New Mexico. AT&SF, laying its tracks west from Kansas, arrived just a few hours ahead of the D&RG crew and won the contract. This shattered Palmer's dream of building a railroad to Mexico—so he turned west toward the silver camps of the San Juan Mountains.

Served by two railroads, Trinidad's depot became a shipping center, sending boxcars of sheep and cattle to eastern markets. Heavy mining equipment and machinery arrived from the East for the silver camps in the San Juans. The town marshal, Bat Masterson, had plenty to do when rambunctious cowboys flooded the town on payday to gamble and quench their thirst at the bars in El Corazon de Trinidad (the Heart of Trinidad). Bat never shot anyone, but he used his fists and boxing skills to toss rowdy lawbreakers into jail. In May 1882, his friend Wyatt Earp rode into town with Doc Holliday after their dustup at Tombstone's O.K. Corral. Bat helped Doc avoid extradition to Arizona to stand trial for murder and sent him on to Denver. Doc spent some time in Denver and then went to Leadville, where the high altitude did not help his case of advanced tuberculosis. Wyatt dealt faro in a Trinidad gambling hall before moving on to boisterous Silverton.

Rich coal deposits were discovered near Trinidad, and hundreds of European immigrants came to work in the mines. A new courthouse, a city hall, a library, and an elegant opera house were built with Trinidad-manufactured bricks or golden sandstone from a nearby quarry. Coal money poured into town, and wealthy bankers, merchants, and coal men built their elegant Victorians on Aristocracy Hill.

The Colorado Coalfield War, believed to be the deadliest labor strike in the history of the United States, began in 1913 and finally ended in 1914. There was a great deal of violence and death, and conditions in the mines did not improve. Many were killed, and the numerous funerals cast a pall of gloom and despair over Trinidad. The arrival of federal troops quelled the violence, but many coal mines closed in the 1920s, and Trinidad's population declined.

During the 1950s, when other towns were demolishing their historic buildings, the town fathers of Trinidad decided instead to save them. Now Main Street winds through historic downtown, Corazon de Trinidad, which is included in a National Historic District. Many of the old streets are paved with the original bricks that were made here and are marked "Trinidad."

The Trinidad History Museum is a complex of restored old homes that contain family heirlooms, photographs, and antique furnishings. The Bloom Mansion is an elaborate Second Empire home built in 1882 by cattle baron Frank Bloom. It is surrounded by century-old trees and flower gardens. The adobe Baca Home was built around 1872 by a Santa Fe Trail entrepreneur. He sold it to early settlers Dolores and Felipe Baca for twenty-two thousand pounds of wool. The Santa Fe Trail Museum is full of artifacts from the days when this was the main route for travel and trade between the United States and Mexico. It contains many relics from those early times, including a fringed buckskin jacket that scout Kit Carson gave to Trinidad's mayor.

Tarabino Inn

Two brothers, John and Barney Tarabino, built their impressive Italianate-style home on a prominent knoll on Chestnut Street in 1907. They moved their large families into the three-story, *U*-shaped brick house, which had two separate wings. The children played on the sun porch and learned their ABCs in the small schoolhouse in the backyard.

The six Tarabino brothers came to Trinidad from Italy in the latter half of the nineteenth century. The eldest, Giovanni (John), arrived in Colorado in 1883 and started a mercantile store in the coal mining community of Engleville, south of Trinidad. He eventually sold his business to the Colorado Fuel and Iron (CF&I) Company and, with his brother Bernardino (Barney), started a general merchandise store in Walsenburg.

In 1899, they opened the Famous Department Store on Trinidad's Main Street, carrying a large variety of clothing and merchandise. Their store was very popular, and the brothers expanded to become the largest mercantile in town. Their four brothers invested in real estate, ranching, and a variety of businesses, and all became very wealthy.

After more than thirty years in Trinidad, John and Barney retired and moved to Santa Monica, California, leaving the Tarabino Real Estate Company to manage their properties. John Tarabino died in 1918, and Barney died just three years later.

The Tarabino home remained in the family until it was sold in the 1960s. It changed hands several times, but it has remained essentially unchanged since its construction over one hundred years ago. There was one important change: the family's outhouses were replaced with indoor plumbing.

The Tarabino Inn, a family home for generations, is now a bed-and-breakfast, home to several friendly spirits. *Courtesy of Wendy Williams.*

Ghosts

The Tarabino Bed and Breakfast Inn is rumored to have several ghosts. Mysterious footsteps are heard on the stairs leading to the second floor, and it's not unusual to catch a whiff of cherry tobacco smoke in the library. Ceiling fans suddenly start whirring when no one has touched the switch, and the oven turns on and off by itself. When the owner, Teresa, was baking, the oven turned on and off so many times that she became really exasperated and ordered, "Cut it out!" The activity immediately stopped.

Occasionally, the entire house is filled with the pleasant, spicy smells of gingerbread and cookies baking. There's even a faint aroma of pine, and the comment, "It smells just like Christmas," is heard often—even in summer. These tantalizing fragrances are noticed when no one is baking in the kitchen.

There's a lot of paranormal activity in an upstairs bedroom, especially near the closet. Several guests have seen the apparition of a "wiry-haired woman quietly rocking in an antique rocking chair." She doesn't speak and slowly fades away when noticed.

A medium who visited the Tarabino Inn sensed the presence of at least seven spirits in the house. She was certain that a man named "Hector" enjoyed smoking his pipe of cherry tobacco in the library. She said two children were playing in different rooms upstairs, and she was certain that the spirit of Barney Tarabino was lingering in the house. She noted an unusual presence in the dining room but assured everyone that the spirits in the house were friendly. She sensed another unknown presence in the Chestnut Suite upstairs and said that two ghosts spent a lot of time walking up and down the front stairs. The owners of the inn have seen the filmy image of a young woman wearing a long, white gown standing at the foot of these stairs. They said, "She was just looking at us with a sad or longing expression—then she faded away."

One guest came down to breakfast and commented that they "had a very busy household." She explained that during the night there had been a gathering of long-gone family members near her room. She added that she

The Tarabino families gathered in this dining room for meals. *Courtesy of Wendy Williams.*

had seen a strange man wander into her room. When she looked through some old newspaper clippings about the Tarabino family, she pointed to a picture of Barney and insisted without hesitation, "That's him!"

A longtime Trinidad resident, F. Dean Sneed, who lived in the Tarabino house when he was a child, wrote about his experiences in a book, *Ghosts of Trinidad and Las Animas County*. His family often heard mysterious, disembodied footsteps, and there were voices throughout the house. Sneed said once he felt a "reassuring hand on my shoulder in the library." He recalled an evening when he was lying on the couch near the stairs. Suddenly, he saw the shadowy figures of two children walking toward him. He said they were quite clear, but he was so terrified that he started screaming loudly. The children vanished just as his mother came running. Sneed said that he always felt protected in the home and he's certain that the spirits in the house were never a threat to him.

4
DEL NORTE

When gold was discovered in the San Juan Mountains in the early 1870s, mining camps sprang up near the rich strikes, and there was an immediate need for food, supplies, and equipment. Because of the mines' remote locations, everything had to be transported by burro or mule pack trains over narrow, treacherous trails, and high mountain passes. There were no roads that could be navigated by heavily loaded freight wagons.

In 1871, the camps in the southern San Juan Mountains could be reached by a rough trail over Stony Pass. J. Cary French and some associates planned a new town that would be a supply center for the mining camps. They selected a site on the sagebrush plains near the Rio Grande del Norte River. Using a mariner's compass, they marked off the streets and city lots, making the main street wide enough for a six-mule freight team to turn completely around.

The town was officially named "Del Norte" on October 23, 1871, and eager merchants soon began arriving with wagons of supplies for the camps. They bought lots, built their stores, and got busy making money. There was little lumber available locally for building, and the nearest sawmill was in Conejos, over fifty miles away. To avoid this long journey, most buildings in Del Norte were constructed of the tough, rhyolite stone that was quarried nearby. Many of these early stone buildings, which range from gray to light pink in color, are still in use more than a century later.

Soon, long pack trains were plodding up the Stony Pass trail, loaded with boxes of dynamite, metal ore cars, steam boilers, kegs of whiskey, quarters of beef, and even whole hogs. Long wooden planks and metal tracks for ore cars were strapped on the burros with one end sticking up in the air, and the opposite end dragging and bumping along. Planks were always cut longer than their designated length to compensate for the amount of wood that would be "dragged off" on the trails. As the long pack trains made their way into the mountains, the metallic screech of the rails on the rocky trail blended with the burros' resentful hee-haws. There was often little rest for the pack animals when they arrived at the camps. They were quickly unloaded, and heavy bags of ore were piled on for the difficult trip back through the mountains. Once the pack trains returned, the bags of ore were loaded into freight wagons and hauled to smelters in Pueblo and Denver.

Del Norte grew quickly, and in 1874, it became the new Rio Grande County's administrative center. By 1881, the Denver & Rio Grande Railroad was rushing to get its tracks laid across the San Luis Valley, hoping to reach the San Juans before the winter storms began. In November, everyone celebrated when the first train chugged into Del Norte, bringing an immediate decrease in the prices of goods, supplies, and mining equipment. Now the railroad would carry ore to the smelters at a much cheaper price than the freighters.

In 1881, three outlaws held up the stage from Del Norte to Silverton, but a sheriff's posse chased them down and captured two of the robbers.

Burro pack trains carried planks of lumber to the mines high in the mountains. *Courtesy of History Colorado.*

Knowing that vigilantes would be waiting with nooses for their prisoners, the sheriff and his men didn't bring them into town until after dark. They locked the outlaws in the jail and went home. During the night, vigilantes broke into the jail, grabbed the prisoners, outfitted them with hemp neckties, and lynched them from a nearby tree. Then they returned the bodies to the jail, where the sheriff found them the next morning—both neatly tucked into their cots, dead.

During its boom, Del Norte's population swelled to around ten thousand, and it even had an opera house and a library. In 1883, George Darby founded the Presbyterian College of the Southwest and built a small observatory on Mount Lookout, which contained the only telescope west of the Mississippi.

Del Norte had several saloons, dance halls, and a red-light district. There were occasional shootings and robberies, and the citizens' vigilante group remained very active. One night, they stormed the jail, intent upon lynching two cattle rustlers, but the intended victims escaped before the vigilantes arrived. Aggravated that their plans for a lynching had gone awry, the

The Windsor Hotel was saved from demolition by Del Norte's citizens. *Courtesy of Wendy Williams.*

necktie party went on a binge, shot up the town, and didn't sober up until they'd killed one of their own members, and wounded several others.

The farms and ranches that developed around Del Norte helped the town survive the depression of 1893 and the closure of the silver mines. Today, farms in the San Luis Valley produce potatoes, barley, and wheat, plus a malt barley that was introduced in the 1950s. Coors Beer buys carloads of this malt barley, grown just for its brewery. The valley's rich soil has produced some spectacular vegetables, like a giant turnip that weighed twenty-one pounds.

WINDSOR HOTEL

The wrecking ball was poised, and the dynamite was ready to demolish the crumbling, old Windsor Hotel, but just a few hours before it was blasted to smithereens, the old derelict was rescued. That happened in 1993 when Dr. Raymond Culp and his wife, Barbara, saved the Del Norte landmark. After buying the hotel, the Culps set up a nonprofit organization to raise funds to rebuild the dilapidated property. Del Norte citizens joined the renovation effort, raising money, and obtaining grants from the state historical fund.

An architect and local contractors began renovations on the historic structure, which had been shut up tight for more than twenty years. Its twenty guest rooms were updated and decorated with nineteenth century–style furnishings, and the Legacy Room Naming Program was started. Donors commemorated their families' heritage with displays of their vintage photos and memorabilia in selected guest rooms. The parlor and dining room were renovated, and the hotel reopened with a gala celebration.

The Windsor Hotel was built in 1874 by Henry Foote, and as Del Norte's largest building, it dominated Grand Avenue. Its lobby bustled with wealthy investors who came to meet mine executives, local ranchers making cattle deals, and farmers arranging sales of their crops. The railroad's arrival in 1881 brought more people, and a vacant room at the Windsor was a rarity, so additions were added in 1884 and 1888.

The hotel survived the Depression and two world wars but was forced to close in the 1970s. It sat vacant, neglected, and deteriorating for the next twenty years until it was within hours of demolition in 1993.

Citizens participated in the Windsor's restoration through the Legacy Room Naming Program. *Courtesy of Wendy Williams.*

Ghosts

After the renovations were completed in 2011, strange things began happening, and everyone wondered if this old hotel had a ghost. Then objects started flying across the kitchen, occasionally hitting someone. The television set in the bar was always turned off at closing, but every morning it was on; the sets in vacant rooms were always turned on.

The historian from the local museum suggested that some answers might be found in their archives. Newspaper clippings told about Maude Heinze, who committed suicide in 1906 at the hotel. The daughter of a wealthy man from Creede, she was an accomplished pianist, who also played the violin. Maude met a handsome brakeman for the Denver & Rio Grande Railroad named Parker, and after a whirlwind romance, the two became engaged. She didn't know that Parker had planned to marry someone else, but they'd had a bad quarrel and a broken engagement.

Then unexpectedly, Parker and his girlfriend buried their differences and resumed their romance. Parker broke Maude's heart when he told her that he didn't love her. The grief-stricken young woman took a room at the Windsor Hotel, using the name Violet Tierri from Ohio. She wrote a letter to her father and another to Parker and mailed them at the post office. Then she went to the Mercantile, where she bought a .38 caliber revolver and a box of bullets. She returned to her room at the Windsor and loaded the gun. After some reflection upon her life, Maude shot herself in the chest, but the shots weren't fatal. Dismayed to find that she was still alive, Maude shakily brought the pistol up to her temple and pulled the trigger. The sound of gunshots brought the hotel staff to Room 209 where they were horrified to find poor Maude drawing her last breath.

Maude's father was notified, and the grief-stricken parent retrieved his daughter's body. Then he tracked down Parker and confronted him. The young man insisted that he'd made a mistake in romancing Maude and repeatedly swore that he had never loved her. This didn't comfort Maude's distraught father, who had to bury his young daughter in the Creede Cemetery.

The ghost of Maude Heinze was stirred up by the renovation of the hotel's twenty rooms, dining room, and fancy parlor. She made her presence known in a variety of disruptive ways and frightened hotel employees. A housekeeper working in room 210 saw the clothes' hangers suddenly start swinging wildly in the closet when there wasn't a draft, and no one else was in the room. The radios and TVs in guests' rooms turned on and off suddenly, and in the bar, glasses went flying off the shelves. When he was closing at night, the bartender often heard the sound of a dripping faucet. This persisted even after the faucet had been turned off several times. Finally, the exasperated bartender shouted, "All right, Maude, I know it's you! Cut it out!" The dripping stopped.

Guests noticed some strange things around the hotel, and their room's doors opened and closed mysteriously. Keys and personal items disappeared often. A woman in room 204 complained that she'd been awakened in the middle of the night by someone running a vacuum directly outside her door. When she threw the door open, the sound stopped, and no one was there. Occasionally, guests staying in room 209 have been awakened by the sound of moans coming from within the room. This stopped immediately when a light was turned on. Other guests have been terrified by the wispy figure of a woman standing near their bedside or drifting about the room.

Several paranormal groups have investigated the activity at the hotel, paying special attention to rooms 209 and 210. One team obtained varying EMF (electromagnetic field) readings in room 209 and recorded the sound of voices that their spirit box picked up in these rooms. Some paranormal investigators speculate that as many as eight spirits are roaming through the Windsor Hotel.

5
SOUTH FORK

In the 1870s, before the expansion of the railroads into the West, passengers, mail, and freight were primarily carried by stagecoaches. The Barlow and Sanderson Company of Missouri transported mail across the country to California, and its stages ran between Denver and Santa Fe. At its height, the company had five thousand mules and horses that were constantly in use, and the company's stages traveled throughout Southern Colorado, linking mining camps. In 1874, South Fork was a welcome stop for stage travelers where they could get out, stretch their cramped muscles, and sniff the fragrant pines.

As the Denver & Rio Grande Railroad advanced across the San Luis Valley, the stage terminus shifted each time a new section of track was completed. In 1881, work was started to extend the D&RG across Cumbres Pass to Del Note, South Fork, Antonito, and Durango. One year later, its task accomplished, the train arrived at the small hamlet of South Fork.

Sheep men and cattle ranchers had claimed this wide, sweeping valley of the Rio Grande River for their herds. Two brothers, O.S. and Charles Galbreath, anticipating a need for lumber for building and fuel, formed the Galbreath Tie and Timber Company. The thick conifer forests around South Fork provided plenty of logs that were cut into planks at their new sawmill. They shipped the lumber throughout the San Luis Valley and eventually to other parts of the West. Galbreath timber was used to shore up tunnel walls in the silver mines of the San Juan Mountains and the gold mines of Summitville. Logs were converted into fuel for steam-operated

Spruce Lodge was built to provide lodging for merchants who came to do business with the Galbreath brothers. *Courtesy of Wendy Williams.*

mining equipment, boilers, and the steam engines of the Denver & Rio Grande Railroad. Countless numbers of trees were cut into railroad ties for the D&RG tracks as the line headed west toward Durango. South Fork grew slowly, with its economy supported by the mill and the railroad.

The Galbreath brothers applied for a U.S. Post Office for South Fork, and when it was approved, they constructed a building to house it. They built a general store, which carried a wide variety of goods, supplies, and equipment and did a brisk business. It was the only store for miles around. Employees of the sawmill and the Galbreath Company were paid in scrip, which they used to purchase groceries and goods at Galbreath's store. Deciding that the town needed a place where visitors could spend the night, the brothers built a small log hotel, which they named Spruce Lodge. When merchants and customers came to South Fork to conduct business with the Galbreaths, the lodge was a convenient overnight accommodation for them.

A rich silver strike was made in the mountains north of South Fork by Nicholas Creede, and by 1891, over $6 million in silver had been taken from its mines. As Creede boomed, the Denver & Rio Grande headed for the new camp, struggling to lay its tracks through a narrow, rocky canyon past Wagon Wheel Gap. Railroad planners complained that there was barely enough room between the cliffs for the North Fork of the Rio Grande River, a primitive wagon road, and the new railroad tracks.

South Fork grew very slowly, but by the early 1900s, the invention of the auto was bringing tourists, eager to explore the mountains and fish in the Gold Medal waters of the Rio Grande.

Through the years, fire was always a threat to South Fork's six hundred year-round residents. In 1967, the Galbreath's lumber mill, which was across the road from Spruce Lodge, was destroyed by a fire, along with an estimated $2 million worth of lumber. Only changing winds kept the huge fire from jumping the road and consuming the Spruce Lodge, the general store, and nearby buildings. Then in 2002, South Fork endured the "Millions Fire," whose threatening flames burned very close to the town. Thirty fire engines were positioned around the community as more than six hundred firefighters battled the blaze; tourists and residents were evacuated for days.

In June 2013, lightning started three separate wildfires near Wolf Creek Pass. The flames were spread by fierce winds, and the three smaller fires merged into one huge fire, which was called the West Fork Complex fire. Once again, more than 1,500 residents and visitors to South Fork and Wagon Wheel Gap were evacuated. As the fire neared town, firefighters predicted South Fork would be lost, but after many difficult days, the flames were finally contained just a mile from the edge of town. Much of the San Juan and Rio Grande National Forests around South Fork were ravaged by this horrific fire, the largest to ever hit this area. It destroyed 110,000 acres, an area of over 114 square miles, and burned for weeks, finally slowed by heavy monsoon rains.

Five years after this disastrous fire, South Fork's economy is slowly recovering. Tourists and summer visitors are returning to fish in the Rio Grande and hike the area's numerous trails. The heavy winter snows attract snowmobilers, and nearby Wolf Creek Ski Area brags that it has "The Most Snow in Colorado," about 430 inches of natural powder annually.

Spruce Lodge

In 1927, O.S. Galbreath and his brother, Charles, built Spruce Lodge in the Rustic architecture style, which developed in the early years of the twentieth century. This style began when the National Park Service started constructing its buildings to harmonize with their natural settings. Structures were built with rock, stone, and local timber that reflected the surrounding landscape. Peeled Engelmann spruce logs, cut in the forest around South Fork, were used in the construction of Spruce Lodge, which accommodated travelers and merchants, who came to conduct business with the lumbermen.

The two-story hotel had a basement with a pool room and barbershop, which was eventually remodeled into a three-bedroom apartment for the owner. Today, there is a lobby, kitchen, restaurant–dining room, and a bathroom on the main floor. There were eight guest rooms on the second floor and two bathrooms. The lodge was one of South Fork's first buildings to get electric lights, and most of the guest rooms have the original push-button light switches and antique fixtures. The chandeliers that once hung in the hotel lobby have been moved to the lodge's small restaurant.

In 1933, when O.S. Galbreath died after a massive heart attack, his brother, Charles, assumed management of the hotel and all the Galbreath enterprises. Around 1936, he had a number of small cabins built near the lodge to accommodate the increasing number of tourists and travelers. In 1946, Charles sold the entire lodge complex to Walt Pickard, who began remodeling the buildings. One night after finishing his work, the plumber left a gas heater running, which started a fire. Two cabins were burned to the ground, and the third was so badly damaged that it could not be repaired.

In 1950, Rickard built the Chalet, which added ten more guest rooms. A small bunkhouse was completed, and the Cook's Cabin, which survived the fire, was improved and became a home for the lodge's cook, who lived there more than thirty years. In 1962, Rickard sold the Spruce Lodge, and it went through several more ownership changes. Jennifer (Dee) and Rob Plucinski purchased Spruce Lodge in 2006, and after completion of the necessary work, it was included in the National Register of Historic Places in 2007.

Ghosts

When the Plucinskis bought the lodge, they heard many stories about its paranormal activity, including the story of a young girl who's often seen peering from an upstairs window. Although the new owners were skeptical, plenty of strange happenings were reported by guests, employees, friends, and construction workers. Upstairs, the guest room doors slammed shut for no reason, and the lights flickered on and off at random. In the kitchen, pots and pans were moved about, and pets often alerted to a presence that humans could not see. Footsteps were heard throughout the building when no one was around, and sometimes when the couple was in a room, the disembodied sounds were with them. When they started remodeling the basement into their living quarters, the paranormal activity increased with many thumps, bumps, and loud footsteps on the stairs.

Once when Rob left the laundry room, he was startled by the shadowy figure of a man standing in the kitchen doorway. While looking through old photographs, he found one of a previous owner, who had died years before. The picture held an eerie resemblance to the apparition he'd seen in the kitchen. On another evening, Rob came face to face with a young blond woman sitting on a pool table in the basement. He said the spirit seemed quite lifelike, just looked at him and then slowly faded away, leaving him quite shaken.

Once Rob distinctly heard a woman's voice whispering in his ear, "Look at me!" Then she said, "Hello." A plumber, who was working alone in the basement, was startled by a voice behind him that asked quietly, "What are you doing?" Prepared to answer and explain the task, he turned around to see—no one. He was alone. The terrified plumber rushed out of the basement, up the stairs, and out of the lodge.

Their skepticism about ghosts gone, Rob and Dee were convinced that their lodge was really haunted. Even after the remodeling was completed, the paranormal activity and mysterious sounds continued. Their young son often talked about his "other mommy," who sat on the side of his bed and talked to him. He described this visitor as an older woman with white hair and glasses. When he was just three years old, the youngster pointed to an upstairs window and asked, "Who dat girl?" His parents saw no one. Other people have reported seeing the image of a little girl at this same window.

Lodge guests have seen shadowy figures in the halls or passing by their door when it's left open. The light bulbs in lamps throughout the hotel are often mysteriously unscrewed, and a large, decorative pile of deer antlers that sits on a table in the lobby is regularly moved from place to place. One couple reported hearing rhythmic drumming sounds in the upstairs hall outside their room, but no one was there. Whenever any painting or routine maintenance jobs are started, the strange activities increase.

Colorado Springs Ghost Hunters investigated the lodge's paranormal activity on two different occasions. Recently, another team of investigators visited the lodge and spent time in several guest rooms. They obtained high

These antlers have been mysteriously moved from place to place by something unseen in Spruce Lodge. *Courtesy of Wendy Williams.*

EMF (electromagnetic field) readings in the Baxterville Room. When they used a spirit box to try to communicate with any unseen entities, they detected several responses and recorded them. The investigators captured a woman's voice and another one that sounded like a man. When the male entity was asked a series of questions, he responded by muttering short phrases. During this investigation, the team used the spirit box to record several different women's voices in various areas of the lodge.

Some guests may have a peaceful night's sleep at the Spruce Lodge, or they might have a few unusual experiences. They might hear some unexplained whispers or footsteps on the old, creaky stairs. Their room door may open quietly, and they might feel a light touch, and they will certainly be aggravated when the batteries in their camera are mysteriously drained.

6
CREEDE

"Holy Moses, I've struck it rich!" yelled Nicholas Creede when his pick smacked into a large rock and hit a fabulous silver deposit. This discovery launched Colorado's last great silver boom. Creede had been prospecting in the Rocky Mountains for twenty years, occasionally making a fairly rich strike and then selling it. He named this 1890 claim the Holy Moses and leased it to financier and railroad magnate David Moffat. Creede resumed prospecting and found two more rich claims nearby, which he called the Amethyst and Ethel.

These strikes brought hundreds of prospectors to the upper Rio Grande Valley, where the new camp of Creede was squeezed between narrow, rocky cliffs on both sides of Willow Creek. Tents and pine shanties popped up along Creede's corkscrew Main Street while some, hoping to beat the exorbitant price of a lot, built their shacks on planks they laid across Willow Creek. This was dangerous because heavy rains and spring's melting snow swelled the creek, overflowing its banks. Every year, residents shuddered as threatening torrents of water roared down the canyon, sweeping cabins and debris along.

The Denver & Rio Grande extended a line to Creede, and the first train chugged into town, jammed with hopeful prospectors, self-important investors, young mining school graduates in long fur coats and new boots. They sat on one another's laps and on the arms of the seats, stood in the aisles, and hung onto the outside platforms. The boom was on, and seemingly overnight, Creede's population exploded to ten thousand. The camp was a melting pot of miners, gamblers, con men, fortune hunters, speculators, and parlor girls. As more silver strikes were made, Creede's "suburbs" of Bachelor, Jimtown, Amethyst, Stumptown, Weaver, and Sunnyside spilled down the narrow gorge and enjoyed brief booms.

Creede was firmly established with its mines, saloons, gambling halls, restaurants, and bawdy houses operating around the clock. Soapy Smith, a notorious con man, ran games of chance at his Orleans Club, as well as handling his duties as Creede's major crime boss.

Bob Ford, the notorious "man who shot Jessie James," opened the Exchange dancehall and saloon, but he was a rowdy, mean drunk, and after shooting out the town's streetlights once too often, he was ordered out of town by the vigilance committee. Bob spent months writing letters to the vigilantes apologizing and begging for permission to return to Creede. He would have been better off staying away from there, because shortly after he returned, his Exchange dancehall was destroyed in the June 1892 fire. After the ashes cooled, Ford opened a tent saloon on the site, but the next day, he was killed by one shotgun blast from Ed O'Kelley. The town's criminal element paid for Ford's funeral and burial in the Shotgun Hill cemetery. A huge crowd gave him a noisy send-off, and the party lasted until the champagne and whiskey ran out. O'Kelley was convicted of second-degree murder, and after serving a few years in Territorial Prison, he was pardoned.

The ladies were popular in Creede, where Lulu Slain and her friend, the Mormon Queen, operated parlor houses competing with several other madams. There was pretty Creede Lillie, Slanting Annie, and Rose Vastine, who was so tall, she was nicknamed "Timberline." Poker Alice Tubbs, a petite blond, was a tough, cigar-chomping, gun-toting gambler who dealt poker and faro in the gambling halls. Sharpshooter Calamity Jane wandered in from South Dakota and made the rounds of the gambling halls, playing poker and proving that she could out-drink any man at the bar.

Bat Masterson joined the rush to Creede, where he managed a saloon and gambling house, instead of hiring on as a lawman. His reputation as a formidable opponent was well known in Creede, where a correspondent for the *St. Louis Globe Democrat* wrote that Bat was "recognized in the camp as the nerviest man of all the fighters here....All the toughs and thugs fear him.... Let an incipient riot start, and all that is necessary to quell it is the whisper, 'Here comes Masterson.'"

Young Jack Dempsey lived in the neighboring mining camp of Bachelor, where his mother operated a boardinghouse. When she groaned about her load of endless work, young Jack promised to buy her a mansion someday, and he kept that promise when he became the World Heavyweight Boxing Champion in 1919.

Creede rebuilt after the 1892 fire, replacing the flimsy, wooden structures with solid brick buildings that were lit by electricity. In 1893, when Mineral County was created by the legislature, a rival town was named county seat, infuriating Creede's citizens. One dark night, a group from Creede stealthily ventured into the rival town, broke into its new, wood frame courthouse and grabbed all the county records. Then they completely dismantled the courthouse itself and hauled all the lumber back to Creede. They reassembled the courthouse on Main Street, and after that escapade, the Mineral County seat remained in Creede. It survived several destructive fires and flash floods that washed many other historic buildings down the canyon.

Hard rock mining kept Creede going through the Depression and two world wars, producing more than $700 million worth of precious metals. In 1985, when the price of silver dropped, the last operating mine, the Homestake, closed. Today, Creede is much quieter than it was when Cy Warman, editor of the *Creede Candle*, wryly wrote, "It's day all day in the daytime, and there is no night in Creede." Now Colorado's last and wildest boom town is a haven for artists and writers, rednecks, and old hippies. Eclectic shops and galleries line Main Street, which runs directly up the dark chasm to the mines, which have over two thousand miles of underground tunnels. The popular Creede Repertory Theater presents musicals, historical dramas, and comedies in the old opera house during the summer.

CREEDE HOTEL

Phillip Zang, a member of a Denver family of brewers, opened the P.H. Zang Brewing Company for Creede's thirsty prospectors, and then he built the Zang Hotel in 1892. There were five guest rooms upstairs and five downstairs, with a dining room and a saloon. None of Creede's hotels was fancy, but this one was considered the finest, and there was never a vacancy.

Zang added an annex with a barbershop where a grimy miner could get a shave and a scrub for twenty-five cents. Just behind the hotel, was the brothel operated by Creede Lil. The hotel was home to Bob Ford, Poker Alice, and Soapy Smith until Bat Masterson's arrival convinced the conman to head for Skagway, Alaska.

Surprisingly, the newly built wood frame hotel survived the disastrous fire of 1892 but was destroyed in the fire of 1906. Phillip Zang died in 1899, and the hotel's operation was taken over by his son, John, and his wife. They ran the hotel well and rebuilt quickly after the fire of 1906. Then disaster struck in the summer of 1911, when a murder and the resulting scandal changed everything.

On June 17, 1911, citizens awoke to the front page of the *Creede Candle* screaming, "Murder! John Zang Shot and Instantly Killed by Mrs. Lefevre at Her Residence." The newspaper article reported that the respected businessman had gone calling upon Mrs. Michael Lefevre, whose husband was out of town. John Zang, who was fifty-five years old, made "unwelcome advances" upon the pretty twenty-five-year-old woman. Mrs. Lefevre said she rebuffed him several times, but her dress was torn when Zang became aggressive. She grabbed a .45 Colt revolver and shot Zang in the face, killing him immediately. "Mr. Zang's side of the story will never be known," the editor of the *Candle* noted somewhat skeptically and predicted that Mrs. Lefevre would be acquitted on grounds of self-defense.

The Creede Hotel hasn't changed much since 1892 when Phillip Zang first opened its doors. *Courtesy of Wendy Williams.*

The article concluded, "May the soul of John Zang rest in peace is the wish of all who knew him."

After a well-publicized trial, the self-confessed murderess was acquitted, but plenty of tongues continued wagging over the notorious murder of John Zang. His wife was so overcome by grief and embarrassment that she attempted suicide. The attempt failed, and after a time, Mrs. Zang resumed her role as a hotel owner. Eight years after her husband's murder, she sold the hotel, remarried, and left Creede for good. Over the intervening years, the hotel had several ownership changes, and its name was changed from the Zang Hotel to the Creede Hotel. Its old saloon has always been a popular hangout for miners, drifters, and local politicians—just as it was a century earlier.

Ghosts

With so many colorful guests at this hotel, it's no wonder a few have decided to stay on. An employee taking photographs of the dining room was astonished when she captured the image of a woman in a Victorian dress in an old mirror. Sometimes footsteps are heard wandering around on the roof, especially during the winter. When someone goes up to look, the snow is pristine, without any visible marks. The aroma of cigar smoke is occasionally evident in the Poker Alice Room, and loud banging is heard in Calamity Jane's when no one is around. Many employees and old-timers say that Phillip Zang, who built the hotel, is still around the premises, checking on his business.

A hotel manager saw the apparition of a woman approach the front desk and chat with the clerk for a few minutes. Then she just faded away. The manager has often heard someone whistling in the old saloon after hours when all the customers are gone. Hotel employees say they often feel like they are being watched while they're working, and there have been occasional glimpses of a shadowy figure, especially early in the morning.

One employee, who was carrying a tray loaded with dishes to the kitchen, was surprised to see the door quietly open before her. She entered the kitchen, and the door closed silently behind her. When this happened, there was no one near.

Guests are asked to record their impressions of their stay in the hotel's journal, and several people have said they heard the sounds of bells in the

Calamity Jane Room. Others "sensed a presence" while they were staying in that room. One guest who spent the night with her husband in the Poker Alice Room wrote that a "ghostly presence" had joined them. She said that they had been awakened several times by the sound of glasses falling off the nightstand. In the morning, there were seven glasses scattered around on the floor near their bed.

Footsteps are often heard on the stairs and in the upstairs hall—of course, no one is there. Occasionally, a wispy white figure is glimpsed upstairs, rounding a corner, and then it disappears. The owner, David Toole, said he's sensed an unseen presence around the hotel and remarked, "I feel that they appreciate me taking care of the place, and they leave me alone."

7
Antonito

You can catch the Cumbres and Toltec Scenic Railroad and travel sixty-four miles over the ten-thousand-foot-high Cumbres Pass and then chug across the yawning Toltec Gorge to Chama, New Mexico. This historic narrow-gauge line was built in 1881 by the Denver & Rio Grande Railroad as part of its operations to support mining in the San Juan Mountains. This railroad is listed in the National Register of Historic Places.

In the early 1800s, huge land grants were given by Spanish viceroys to their citizens to encourage settlement of this remote, unknown region. Despite frequent attacks by the Navajos and other Indian tribes, Spanish settlers came north from New Mexico to the vast San Luis Valley. They built tiny adobe villages, planted their crops, and dug irrigation ditches to carry water from the river to their fields of beans and corn. They brought herds of sheep from New Mexico, and this eventually developed into an important industry for this area. Some settlers owned very large herds of as many as fifty thousand animals.

After the Civil War ended, the Homestead Act of 1862 was enacted. The act gave 160 acres of land to anyone who would settle on it and farm for at least five years. As more Anglos came to the San Luis Valley, two ferries were established that crossed the Rio Grande, while another was built on the Culebra River.

Antonito grew rapidly, and it soon dominated the area, becoming a railroad and commercial center for the surrounding farmers and ranchers. Large numbers of sheep were shipped to eastern markets, and the depot was often crowded with wool brokers.

This water tower supplied the coal-fired engines of the Denver & Rio Grande Railroad in 1879. *Courtesy of Wendy Williams.*

Antonito had once been a tiny border sheep camp called San Antonio Junction. When the Denver & Rio Grande selected this site for a rail center and built a depot out of lava rock, people saw the commercial opportunities. If they wanted the business generated by the railroad, they would have to leave Conejos and move a few miles south to Antonito. Most did just that, and soon the tiny town along the railroad tracks had a population of around one thousand. They were proud that the oldest church in Colorado, Our Lady of Guadalupe Catholic Church, built in 1857, is nearby.

Two Spanish-language newspapers were printed in Antonito, and the SPMDTU (Sociedad Proteccion Mutua de Trabajadores Unidos) was organized in 1900. This Society for the Mutual Protection of United Workers soon had more than one thousand members, most of whom lived in this southern part of the San Luis Valley. The benevolent fraternal organization provided direct benefits through a members' insurance program and gave them a voice against discrimination toward Spanish-speaking workers. The large beige headquarters building in Antonito, constructed in 1925, is still in use, and its members extend helping hands to those in need.

During the 1920s, many Japanese moved into this valley and began raising lettuce, cabbage, cauliflower, and garden crops. Potatoes and sugar beets became very important in the agricultural economy, which still sustains the San Luis Valley. Most visitors to Antonito today come to ride the narrow-gauge Cumbres & Toltec Scenic Railroad, which runs May through October. This is no luxury excursion, and visitors experience the train as western travelers did more than a century ago. Antonito is brightened by the numerous large, colorful murals that have been painted on buildings, water towers, and silos by Fred Haberlein. A native of this area, Haberlein has completed over 130 murals single-handedly, which is more than any other U.S. artist.

STEAM TRAIN HOTEL

The big, black safe from the local bank is still sitting in the lobby of the Steam Train Hotel. It dates back to the days when it protected the money of farmers, wool brokers, and sheep men of Antonito. This two-story, red brick building on the corner of Fourth and Main Street was a multipurpose structure with a lobby and the bank on the first floor and hotel rooms on the second. They were reached by a staircase built on the outside of the building. Like many buildings of its time, the Steam Train was situated on a large corner lot with two entrances. Some buildings of the late 1890s and early twentieth century were constructed with three stories. There would be a bank, saloon, restaurant, or mercantile stores on the first floor; office space that was often rented by doctors, lawyers, and mining or utility companies on the second; and the top floor usually contained hotel rooms or apartments.

The safe remained in the building when the bank closed, and it is eye-catching. Large and black, with its name in bright gold letters, its heavy vault door swings open to reveal rows of large, old-fashioned safe deposit boxes. Interesting old ledgers are stored here, as well as rolls of aged documents. This building was constructed in 1911 and was located across the street from the original train depot.

Today, the Steam Train Hotel provides accommodations to travelers and those who come to ride the historic Cumbres & Toltec Railroad to Chama, New Mexico. The hotel has been refurbished and offers twelve guest rooms, decorated with an interesting assortment of antiques and southwestern

Many Steam Train Hotel guests ride the Cumbres &Toltec Scenic over ten thousand feet high Cumbres Pass to Chama, New Mexico. *Courtesy of Wendy Williams.*

furnishings. The attached building on the hotel's east side is much older than the brick bank building and was once a brothel. Its narrow halls and few windows set deep within its thick adobe walls show that it must be several hundred years old.

Ghosts

Investigators have reported a strange form of paranormal activity here that is usually seen as a gray mist or a drifting cloud. This cloud has been seen floating through the halls, and occasionally it moves toward the old, inoperable elevator shaft. This type of paranormal phenomenon is rare, and some say it's an entity manifesting itself in an unusual way. Two rooms are believed to have their own resident ghosts that rarely venture out into the rest of the hotel.

The presence of several spirits has been noted by the manager and others familiar with this old building. Doors open and close on their own, and objects mysteriously disappear or are moved about. When no one is present upstairs, loud footsteps can be heard walking about overhead. This sound is noticed most often by a person who is standing in the lobby below the room believed to be haunted by a very active ghost.

The manager has been puzzled by a strange phenomenon that has occurred several times. The lobby has been cleaned, the floor swept, and first floor locked up for the night. The next morning, the hotel manager finds muddy footprints and loose dirt directly in front of the safe. She said that there is always enough that she has to sweep it up with a broom and dustpan. This room is always locked at night, and no one has access to it.

8
DURANGO

General William Palmer planned Durango in 1880, and it was to be a rail shipping center, sending supplies, food, and equipment to Silverton. The mines would ship their silver and gold ore to the smelters at Denver and Pueblo, and this cheaper transportation would help develop the mining industry.

The town site of Durango was laid out by the railroad's survey crew, and it was named after the city in Mexico. Like Colorado Springs, businesses, hotels, and retail stores would be on Main and Second Streets. Third Avenue would be the residential boulevard with rows of green trees where homes, churches, and schools were far from the noise and dust of the business district. Land was set aside for parks, churches, a school, city hall, and even a future county administration building.

City lots full of sunflowers, sagebrush, and scattered pines were sold for $200, but the price quickly increased to $300, while the best lots were selling for $1,000. Wood frame buildings went up rapidly as the plans for a business district built of fire-deterring rocks or bricks were abandoned. Lumber was scarce, even with six sawmills, and the local brickyard could not keep up with the demand. Within one year, Durango had a population of 2,400, with 134 businesses, 5 lumberyards, 20 saloons, and 10 real estate firms.

The railroad arrived in Durango on August 5, 1881, and work began on a forty-five-mile extension up Animas Canyon to Silverton. The tracks were completed in eleven months, and the Denver & Rio Grande steamed triumphantly into Silverton on July 10, 1882.

One of the first engines of the Denver & Rio Grande Railroad. *Courtesy of History Colorado.*

By the end of 1881, Durango had five newspapers, one of which, the *Record*, was guided by Caroline Romney. She'd hustled down from Leadville in 1880 with her printing press, anxious to publish Durango's first daily newspaper. Described as slightly plump and very pretty, Mrs. Romney was immediately immersed in local politics and intrigues. She was an ardent booster of Durango, praising it as the "new city in the wilderness" and the "new wonder of the Southwest." She advocated for women's rights, campaigned actively for women's suffrage, and insisted that all businesses should be closed on Sunday. Romney became embroiled in squabbles with Denver journalists, who criticized Durango's "lurid lawlessness" and scornfully referred to it as "the sagebrush metropolis." In the 1881 election, the *Record* urged Durango's citizens to vote against retaining Denver as the state's capital. The new boom town was touted as the "Denver of Southern Colorado," and there were predictions that five thousand people would call it home by 1883.

As the town grew, crime increased, but Durango did not have a jail for captured criminals. There were stagecoach robberies, holdups, and horse thieves, and cattle rustlers raided herds and evaded capture by jumping across the New Mexico border. Territorial disputes between outlaw gangs spilled over into Durango, and the notorious Stockton-Eskridge gang was constantly fighting with the rival Simmons gang from Farmington, New Mexico. One morning, about twenty-five armed Simmons horsemen took up positions on the mesa east of Durango. Their rifle bullets suddenly began spraying the town, digging into the dirt streets and wooden sidewalks as the Stockton-Eskridge men returned the gunfire from the Railroad Street saloons. Durango's citizens fled for cover, cowering in their homes and shops, but surprisingly, no one was seriously hurt.

On Easter Sunday in April 1881, Henry Moorman walked into a saloon and announced that he was going to kill someone. When he did shoot an innocent cowboy, vigilante justice prevailed, and the murderer was hauled outside town and swung into the hereafter by the "Committee of Safety." William Folsom, a young dentist who'd just arrived in town, described the sight: "He was hung on a pine tree across from my office.…This was a hard country then."

This hanging and the gunfight between the outlaw gangs spurred the lethargic city council into action, and members got busy establishing a stronger city government. A vigilance committee was appointed, a town marshal selected, a police force set up, and police judges chosen. Durango established the framework of city government and implemented a source of revenue to pay for it. A solid jail was built, and the city council decided that prisoners would receive a Spartan diet of coffee, bread, meat, and water.

The only legal hanging in Durango took place on June 23, 1882. George Woods had killed an unarmed man in the Pacific Club Saloon, and he was tried, found guilty, and sentenced to be hanged just one month after the murder. His execution was attended by more than three hundred spectators, many of whom brought their children and had a family picnic. The hanging took place across the street from where the Strater Hotel now stands. When Durango became too uncomfortable for outlaws and gangs, they headed north to Silverton to cause trouble there. After 1883, the city marshal reported that drunkenness, disturbing the peace, and gambling were Durango's only real crime issues. He said he spent more time rounding up stray dogs and burros, small boys, and drunks than he did chasing down criminals.

Many of Durango's saloons and gambling halls were congregated in one block off Main Avenue, and they operated around the clock. The sporting houses were conveniently located around the corner from the saloons. This red-light district existed in spite of the city fathers' prohibition of bawdy houses and gambling. Virtue soon gave way to practicality—gambling and women were sources of revenue for the city government. The madams who ran the bawdy houses paid a monthly "fine" of $235, and their working girls paid them "rent." Durango had twice as many saloons as churches, and saloon owners paid an annual $400 fee to operate. Legitimate businesses paid much lower license fees, and saloon owners protested loudly at city council meetings. These confrontations continued for years, but no changes were made.

Durango was a lively place for families in the 1880s. Wealthy men who had made money in the silver mines settled in town and brought their families from the East. Mining engineers, managers from the smelter, and local businessmen, as well as U.S. Army officers from Fort Lewis, came to Durango. This well-to-do group built their large homes on Third Avenue and kept a busy social calendar of balls, dances, and picnics. There was dancing and skating, while plays and concerts were performed by local drama clubs. Picnics on the river and the popular strawberry festival drew hundreds of families; the Chicago Comedy Club performed to sold-out crowds every year when the troupe came to town. When Robinson's Circus arrived in 1883, even the Utes showed up for the big parade; the tall men with their wives and giggling youngsters lined up along Main Street with everyone else. Mrs. John Jackson Haggert recalled that "when the elephants came along, the Indians who usually make no demonstration, simply doubled up with laughter and rolled on the ground and howled, and then crowded around the amazing beasts."

The citizens of Silverton were not happy when their smelter was moved to Durango where coal was readily available, and the railroad was nearby. Operations were set up on the west bank of the Animas River, and the smelter was enlarged, becoming the nucleus of a regional smelting center. The smelter would become Durango's chief industry for the next fifty years, employing more men than any other company. Durango's citizens cheerfully tolerated its noise and smelly smoke because it brought more jobs and business to their town. By the 1890s, it would be Colorado's ninth-ranked smelter, and several large coal mines operating close to town added to the smoke. The coal mines fueled the railroads and smelters, and generated power for electricity, while creating a black cloud of smoke over Durango.

On July 1, 1889, a fire devastated several blocks of the business and residential districts, destroying many commercial buildings, homes, three churches, the courthouse, city hall, and the new jail. Panicked residents fled from town and watched the fire from a nearby mesa until the volunteer firemen got the flames under control. The following day, there was a meeting of the town's citizens, and they decided to begin raising money to rebuild.

After the rubble was cleared away, the wooden, false-fronted buildings of the frontier days were gone. The business district was rebuilt to look like the commercial capital of the Southwest. Within just a year, Durango rose phoenix-like from the ashes with city blocks of new, brick commercial buildings that rivaled those of Denver and Pueblo. By 1890, the town had horse-drawn trolleys, which ran the length of Main Avenue, often stopping at the Strater and other large hotels along their route, picking up and dropping off passengers. By 1900, Durango was the first city in Colorado to have electricity-powered street cars.

By the turn of the century, Durango had become a vacation destination after the creation of the San Juan National Forest in 1905 and Mesa Verde National Park in 1906. It was the largest town on the Western Slope and growing steadily until the Depression closed the smelter. It was reopened during World War II to process vanadium, a key component in developing a rust-resistant stronger grade of steel. Vanadium mining boomed, and it wasn't until the war ended that it became known that uranium was also being mined. This blasted Durango into the Atomic Age. By 1948, the vanadium mill at Durango was a major uranium producer, running around the clock. The workforce soared, and once again the smelter was the area's major employer. The uranium was used in the Manhattan Project, and the plant operated until 1963. In 1984, Congress ordered the EPA and the Department of Energy to remove the smelter's huge brick smokestack and clean up the piles of radioactive tailings produced by the vanadium processing.

Durango has prospered as the commercial and tourism center of La Plata County, and it is the gateway to Mesa Verde, the Four Corners region, and the San Juan Mountains. The Durango and Silverton Railroad has been in continuous operation since 1881, and it is a National Historic Landmark and a designated National Historic Civil Engineering Landmark. This train has transported over $300 million in precious metals, and now it carries over 200,000 passengers a year.

STRATER HOTEL

Henry Strater thought Durango needed a really fine, first-class hotel, and he was just the man to build it. This twenty-year-old pharmacist from Cleveland was certain that a high-caliber establishment would add some class to Main Avenue. Despite his grand ideas, Stater had a few strikes against him: first, he had no money; second, he had no established credit; third, he was too young to enter into a legal contract; and fourth, he had no experience building or operating a hotel.

Never one to give up, Henry stretched the truth about his age and borrowed money from the bank. Then he convinced his wealthy relatives to loan him enough cash to buy a corner lot on Main Avenue for the hotel. He began construction in the summer of 1887.

The four-story, red brick hotel took up an entire block when it was completed late in 1887. Built in the popular Victorian Eclectic style, it looked just like a fancy wedding cake, with contrasting hand-carved, white sandstone–bracketed cornices, pediments, and window sills. There was a decorative cupola on the corner of the roof that overlooked Main Avenue, and elegant clothing and fine merchandise were displayed in the first floor's large glass windows.

The hotel opened in 1888, and guests were impressed by the spacious lobby, crystal chandeliers, and fine antiques. Gentlemen could have their locks trimmed or their whiskers groomed in the barbershop while a harpist played soft melodies. There were two bathing rooms with tubs where miners and cowboys joined the wealthy guests, scrubbing and soaking for only twenty-five cents.

The Strater was one of the first hotels to use an "annunciator," a bell system that connected each room to the main desk. A certain number of rings from a room signaled a need for ice water, bath water, or firewood. Despite its elegance, young Strater had forgotten closets for guest rooms and had given no thought to the importance of modern plumbing. In the absence of water closets, wealthy guests had to use a chamber pot or traipse to the three-story outhouse attached to the back of the hotel.

The hotel became a winter retreat for some locals who closed up their homes and moved in for the snow season. They toasted their toes at the wood-burning stoves in each room and enjoyed the comfortable furniture. A few of the finest rooms even had pianos.

The Strater became the favorite place for social events, and the society columns of the newspapers faithfully reported every dinner, dance, masked ball, and debut. Durango's first opera house was inside the Strater, and in addition to opera, a variety of performers appeared, including Tom Thumb, the dwarf, and his troupe. Durango ladies and their children were invited to the hotel for special occasions where the youngsters were

The Strater Hotel, with its cornices and gingerbread trim, is a prominent Durango landmark. *Courtesy of Wendy Williams.*

entertained while their mothers were engrossed in card games of whist and euchre. Often, string trios played chamber music and entertained guests during the Sunday dinner hour.

Strater leased his hotel to H. Rice, but the two men soon had a bitter dispute. They were unable to resolve their problems, so Strater built a competing hotel right next door. When completed, the new, three-story hotel, called the Colombian, had forced-air heating and was advertised as "the only first-class hotel in Durango." The Silver Panic of 1893 brought hard times, and business fell off, although both hotels managed to keep their doors open by lowering their rates. They competed for business until 1895, when the depressed economy put both into foreclosure. In 1902, the bank sold the two hotels to Hattie Mashburn and Charles Stilwell, who merged them, keeping the Strater name.

The quarters for the maids and waitresses were on the fourth floor at the rear of the building; while the floor's front rooms were rented to traveling salesmen and permanent bachelor boarders. Some of the girls offered more to traveling salesmen than "clean towels," and Miss Hattie had her hands full trying to keep order. Because of the shenanigans and monkey business that went on, the salesmen gave this floor its special name, "Monkey Hall." Even though it was off-limits, curious gents and local dandies, armed with pocket flasks of white lightning, often found their way up the back stairs to the rooms of the friendly girls.

One evening, someone in Monkey Hall fired a shot, and it was followed by a loud scream. The manager and a porter, named Enos, bounded up the stairs to confront a crowd of merrymakers. The gun had been fired accidentally, frightening one of the girls. Terrified, she'd thrown her arms around her older "sugar daddy" and refused to let go. Now this gentleman was one of the hotel's best customers, referred to as "Mr. Smith." A traveling salesman and devout churchgoer, with a wife and children at home, Mr. Smith liked to have fun when he was on the road. Now caught in the act, he was terribly embarrassed and struggled to free himself from the girl's stranglehold. His panicked playmate was a pretty blond showgirl nicknamed "Kitty in Boots" because she always wore little fur-trimmed boots. As curious guests crowded onto the fourth floor, Mr. Smith shouted desperately to the porter, "Enos, Take her away! Take her away! I have a reputation! Think of my reputation!" The onlookers were convulsed with laughter, and from that day on, he was known around Durango as "Reputation Smith."

During Prohibition, the Strater became the headquarters of a bootlegger and his wife, who smuggled spirits across the border from Mexico. They hid the liquor in two large cars, which they painted white with red crosses to disguised them as ambulances. They left the vehicles outside town, sneaked the booze into the hotel, and invited local playboys to their room to sample their wares. One night when they caught one of the hotel porters helping himself to a few bottles of bathtub gin, they took some shots at him but missed. As the terrified thief dashed from the hotel, another guest threw a string of firecrackers after him. The racket drew quite a crowd to the Strater, and no one even missed the porter, who hopped the first train out of town.

In 1926, banker Earl Barker Sr. and a group of Durango businessmen bought the hotel and began renovating and updating the thirty-nine-year-old building. They installed modern bathrooms, air conditioning, and telephones but retained the hotel's Victorian charm. Eventually, Barker Sr. bought out his partners and operated the hotel successfully until 1954 when his son, Earl Jr., and his wife, Jentra, took over. While on a trip to Georgia, they found an authentic Victorian bed in an antique store. It gave them the idea of furnishing several of the larger hotel rooms with vintage pieces. They rented a truck and filled it with antiques purchased on the drive back to Colorado. This was the beginning of the Strater's collection of American Victorian walnut antiques. Earl and Jentra's son, Rod, has added pieces, and today the Strater has the world's largest collection of walnut

The Strater Hotel has the world's largest collection of dark walnut antiques displayed throughout the hotel. *Courtesy of Courtesy of Wendy Williams.*

antiques. Glass showcases filled with antique collectibles, like the gold-plated commemorative Winchester rifle and a real Stradivarius violin, are displayed throughout the hotel.

The lobby regained its elegance when it was furnished with these expensive antiques; plush velvet draperies, and chandeliers that came from the old La Plata County Court House. The front desk was from a London pub, while the back portion is an antique walnut buffet with an ornate carving of Bacchus, the god of wine. Hand-printed reproductions of the original wallpaper and fine woodwork decorate the entire hotel.

Over the years, the hotel has entertained many celebrities and important people: Presidents Gerald Ford and John Kennedy, Robert Kennedy and movie stars: Robert Redford, Chevy Chase, Michael Keaton, and Audie Murphy. Lowell Thomas, the renowned reporter, author, radio commentator, and world traveler, took a suite of rooms and broadcast his NBC program from the Strater. Will Rogers was a big favorite in Durango and stayed at the Strater just three weeks before he and his pilot, Wiley Post, were killed in a plane crash in Alaska in 1935.

Today, each of the ninety-three guest rooms is furnished as it was in the 1890s, and they are part of a special Room Dedication Project. Eventually, every room will be named after individuals, families, and institutions that have been important in the development of Durango and the surrounding area. In 2012, room 222 was dedicated to author Louis L'Amour and his wife, Kathy, who always spent several weeks in the summer here. They rented this room, which is directly over the Diamond Bell Saloon, because Louis said the honkytonk tunes helped him set the mood for his Westerns. The wooden drop-leaf table where he wrote the Sackett series is still there. In August 2012, twenty-four years after L'Amour died in 1988, the Strater Hotel and the Friends of the Durango Library placed a plaque on the wall by room 222, designating it a National Literary Landmark. Rod Barker, owner of the Strater, said, "This was always the Louis L'Amour Room," and the author's widow recalled, "This became our summer home. What a sweet day for me." There are only 122 other designated literary sites in this country, and Ernest Hemingway, Mark Twain, Robert Frost, and Edgar Allan Poe have been similarly honored.

Ghosts

When hotel owner Rod Barker was asked about the hotel's ghosts, he laughed and said, "We're 112 years old! I guess we're entitled to a few ghost stories." An incident that was reported in the October 24, 1999 *Durango Herald* took place one night when Barker was working at the front desk. A young couple who'd checked in earlier rushed down the stairs with their suitcases and said that they were leaving. The woman was obviously frightened and swore that she'd seen an apparition dressed like a saloon girl drifting around their room. The husband agreed to stay if they were given a different room, but his wife was adamant, "We're leaving!" They did.

Another couple who stayed at the hotel on their honeymoon snapped some pictures of each other in their room. One of these photos showed the husband sitting on the bed with a mysterious shadowy figure standing behind him that no one could explain. Many photographs taken in different guest rooms show unexplained orbs floating about. Rod Barker said, "My sister claims she has seen two ghosts: one is a little girl who likes to run around and the other one is a man in the theater." He continued, "She was walking through the theater one night when she noticed a man in period costume standing up on the stage. She turned around for a second look, and he was gone. She's convinced it was Henry Strater."

There are three apparitions that have been seen around the hotel many times. A man dressed like a railroad engineer walks through the lobby at different times of the day and night. A little girl dashes around the halls and suddenly disappears, and there have been many reports of a child running about in the banquet room. People walking through the alley next to the hotel have seen the ghostly figure of a man in a white shirt standing on the railroad tracks. He vanishes suddenly.

There's been a lot of paranormal activity on the fourth floor, where several shadowy figures have been seen in the hall. Stealthy footsteps are heard in the halls, and the lights flicker on and off. The electrical wiring has been updated, so an antiquated system isn't the cause. The doors of rooms suddenly bang shut or swing open when no one is around, and there's no draft to blame. Other times a door just slowly opens to an empty, quiet hall. Some housekeepers refuse to work alone on this upstairs floor. Several said that they sense a threatening spirit, while other employees have seen the transparent figure of a woman dressed in white. Strange images have been glimpsed in the antique mirrors, and occasionally a wispy figure glides through a room. One maid was working alone in a guest room when she was touched on the shoulder, but when she turned around, no one was there. Other housekeeping employees said they, too, have been startled by a touch when they were alone. Most of these incidents have occurred on the upper floor.

Rochester Hotel

The foundation of the Rochester Hotel was laid in 1890 on a piece of land that was owned by Alexander Hunt, a former territorial governor. He sold the property to E.T. Peeples, who in turn sold the unfinished building to a group of Durango businessmen. They opened it as the Peeples Hotel. The rectangular brick hotel had thirty-three guest rooms on the second floor, and there was a popular restaurant on the first floor. During the 1893 depression, the hotel was sold to Jerry Sullivan, who managed to stay in business, running it as a boardinghouse for railroad men and miners.

When the economy improved, tourists and businessmen began arriving again on the train, and they stayed at the Peeples. Sullivan sold the hotel in 1905 to Mary Francis Finn, who renamed it the Rochester Hotel. She enlarged the lobby by extending it out to the sidewalk; then she installed modern inside bathrooms for hotel guests. Mary Finn sold the hotel, and it changed hands several more times, but as the years passed, it was neglected and needed repairs.

In 1992, the Rochester Hotel was purchased by Diane and Frederick Wildfang and her son, Kirk Komick. They did an extensive renovation, retaining much of the original woodwork and hardware. Now hotel guests enjoy afternoon tea in the remodeled lobby. The staircase leading to the second floor has its original 1890s banisters, and the antiques from the hotel's early days are still in use.

There are fifteen guest rooms with private baths, high ceilings and the original transoms above the doors. Each room is named for a movie filmed in the Durango area. Movie posters advertising *Across the Wide Missouri*, the Jimmy Stewart classic *Naked Spur* and the comedy *City Slickers*, plus many other favorites, are framed in bright marquee lights and line the hallways. The Leland House across the street, a 1927 brick building, was also remodeled by the Wildfangs and Komick and offers twelve guest apartments.

Ghosts

During the 1993 renovations, several contractors quit, saying that working in the old building made them very uncomfortable. "It just didn't feel right—I was always looking over my shoulder," said one. Frederick Wildfang, a local historian and co-owner, said that guests and employees have been reporting strange happenings in two of the rooms for many years. "We have indications that the hotel is haunted," he said in the October 29, 2009 issue of the *Durango Telegraph*. He continued, "It has been on national TV and the hotel is now on the register of the '100 Most Haunted Hotels in America.'" Wildfang investigated the hotel's history and talked to the local police and fire department before buying it. He remarked, "The hotel has been open since the 1890s, and there were a lot of incidents during Prohibition.... Second Avenue wasn't a street you would walk down at night. This was a rough end of town."

The apparition of a woman wearing a Victorian wedding dress or a long, fancy nightgown has been glimpsed in room 204. Others have seen her drifting around in peek-a-boo lingerie. This is the John Wayne Room, and

Wildfang says, "We get calls every Halloween to rent out this room. People come from all over the country." This room always interests paranormal investigators and ghost hunters.

When longtime jazz-blues musician and actor Bill Henderson checked into room 204, he soon asked for a different room. He insisted that the Duke himself had spoken to him from the TV set. Henderson, whose movie credits go back to 1972 and include roles in *City Slickers* and *Lethal Weapon 4*, was quite unnerved by the experience. Although 204 has the most activity, guests in other rooms at the Rochester have noticed their toiletries and personal items have been rearranged or misplaced. Most things reappear. Doors that were left unlocked by employees are mysteriously locked—from inside the room.

9
SILVERTON

In 1860, a small group of prospectors led by Jim Baker ventured into the southern San Juan Mountains looking for gold. They found a little gold dust in the creeks despite the pesky black sand that clogged their gold pans. Cold weather and snow drove them from the camp they called Baker's Park, and no white men ventured into the San Juan Mountains for the next decade.

In 1870, a few prospectors returned with some knowledge of geology, and now they knew that the pesky black sand was silver. The gold dust in the creeks came from veins in hard rock that were high above. Looking for the gold sources, they climbed the peaks around Baker's Park, going above the tree line to twelve thousand feet in altitude. Here, three prospectors discovered silver deposits and a wide vein of gold. They began mining, and news of their discovery spread fast.

Prospecting was impossible during the winter, but in the spring of 1871, prospectors found some exposed cliffs and rocky peaks crisscrossed by wide bands of silver. As more prospectors trespassed on the Utes' territory in the San Juan Mountains, the Indians attacked them. By the end of 1872, there was real trouble brewing. Negotiations began between the two factions, and after weeks of discussions and arguments, the Brunot Agreement was made in September 1873. The Utes gave up the San Juans, including all of the mining areas and lands surrounding the mountains. They kept some land on the west side of the Rockies as a reservation for the Northern Utes while others went to a reservation in the southwest corner of the territory. The

Mine structure in the Red Mountain District that produced millions of dollars in silver. *Courtesy of Wendy Williams.*

Brunot Agreement opened the mineral-rich San Juan Mountains to mining and brought hundreds of prospectors to look for wealth on the rugged peaks. Between 1870 and 1874, 80 percent of all claims filed in the San Juan Mountains were for silver—not gold.

In 1872, a town site was laid out in the valley, and the streets were named after the area's first prospectors. The town may have gotten its name when a prospector joked, "We may not have gold, but we've got silver by the ton!" Free lots were offered to anyone who would put up a "respectable building" in the new town of "Silverton," as ragged tents and brush shelters were slowly replaced by a rough log cabins. As more strikes were made, mining camps developed at the mouths of gulches that led up to the high peaks.

In 1874, the legislature created San Juan County and named Silverton the county seat. The summer of 1875 saw Silverton's first newspaper, the *La Plata Miner*, roll off the press. This was a victory for editor John Curry, who had packed his old 1839 printing press on a pack mule and walked sixty miles over steep Stony Pass, carrying his printing supplies. There was plenty of news in this booming town, which in just two years, had a drugstore, a meat market, two general stores, an assay office, an ore reduction works, and several saloons. In 1876, Silverton had a brass band, a baseball team, and the first fire department in the San Juans. There was no church, but the town had a grand racetrack, where there was plenty of betting.

By 1878, the only roads that led to Silverton and the larger mining camps were pack trails.

Eastern newspapers described the San Juan Mountains as "the wealthiest district in the wide west," but this did not bring wealthy investors to develop new mines. There was no economical way to get rich gold and silver ore to the smelters, and production and transportation costs were higher than profits. By the 1880s, Otto Mears had built a system of toll roads through the mountains connecting the camps, but some were barely navigable by wagons or stagecoaches.

Silverton attracted con men, thieves, and shady ladies who worked in the brothels on Blair Street. By 1875, this had become Colorado's most notorious red-light and gambling district with around forty saloons and dance halls and eighteen brothels. There were twenty-seven gambling dens, and one of the most popular was the Laundry, where "If you went in with any money, you came out clean!"

In 1879, the town fathers passed a number of ordnances against "bawdy houses," prostitutes, and gambling halls. Bawdy houses were fined $50 to $300 per month, while prostitutes paid $10 to $100 per month. "Fines" were issued on schedule and paid every month by the working girls or the madam. Gambling halls were charged $25 per month. The stiff license fees paid by brothel owners, prostitutes, and dance hall girls defrayed the costs of city and county government, and Silverton's coffers grew full. This revenue from vice made property taxes unnecessary, making the town fathers happy.

Many of Silverton's citizens and lawmen owned large saloons and elegant bordellos, often masquerading as dance halls. They operated twenty-four hours a day, seven days a week. When a dance hall or a large bordello changed hands, the occasion was celebrated with a grand ball. The affair was described in the *Silverton Standard*, and the article would always conclude, "The lack of space prevents us from giving the names of the Silverton elite that attended." Naturally, the "elite" did not want their names listed as attendees of a celebration at a bordello.

These gentlemen split their social obligations between Blair Street events and the numerous activities of fraternal organizations that were promoted by their wives. The newspapers used plenty of ink describing the fraternal

Silverton's Cowboy Band of 1880 was very popular and traveled around Colorado performing. *Courtesy of History Colorado.*

grand balls, picnics, and social gatherings, just as they described all the Blair Street celebrations. Brothel owners and casino operators were respected members of the Elks, Odd Fellows, Fraternal Order of the Eagles, Masons, Woodmen of the World, and the Knights of Pythias, while their wives were active in the Women of Woodcraft and Eastern Star.

Silverton's citizens were anxious for the Denver & Rio Grande to arrive and watched anxiously as the railroad survey crew worked its way up Animas Canyon in 1879. The rugged mountains and narrow, rocky gorge made their work very difficult, and the crew often to be belayed down steep cliffs. During the fall of 1881, they began building the roadbed and laying the tracks north until deep snow stopped all work. Avalanches often swept down the slopes, across the canyon, tearing up the newly laid tracks.

After the spring snows melted, work resumed, and the railroad tracks slowly approached the town. On July 13, 1882, when the first D&RG train chugged triumphantly into Silverton, it was met by two brass bands and a huge crowd. The arrival of the railroad brought less expensive food and supplies, and the cost of transporting ore to the smelters was cheaper. This brought mining investors and businessmen, whose new enterprises boosted the economy.

The bitter cold winters piled up snow burying houses so deep, that people made trapdoors in their roofs so they could get inside. In 1884, heavy snow drifts and an avalanche blocked the railroad tracks and isolated the town for seventy-three days. Crews from Durango and Silverton, using picks, shovels, and dynamite, worked for days to break an opening in the eighty-four-foot-thick wall of compacted snow and ice blocking the canyon. When the train finally came whistling into town, it was met by a weeping, cheering crowd, who'd been facing starvation. Their shared food was gone, and there were only a few cups of flour left.

During the Silver Decade of the 1880s, Colorado became the nation's number-one silver producer, more than $14 million a year. Between 1890 to 1893, silver production increased to $20 million per year, but the "silvery San Juans" became victims of their own success. For several years, the government had been purchasing silver, which maintained its price. When they produced more silver than the market could absorb, prices gradually fell. After Congress repealed the Sherman Silver Purchase Act in 1893, the price of silver collapsed, mines closed and the Silver Kings, who'd ridden the silver wave to wealth and prominence, were ruined. Jobs were lost, foreclosures began, property values fell, savings disappeared as banks and businesses failed. Without the mines, the railroads couldn't pay their debts, and coal mining dwindled. As Silverton's mines closed, 1000 men were thrown out of work, and many left town to look for work elsewhere.

Silverton's economy improved during World War I since many gold and silver mines also produced lead, zinc, and strategic metals. The soldiers were coming home from the war when the Spanish influenza struck in October 1918 and wiped out entire families in one day. There were so many deaths that the undertaker was overwhelmed, and bodies stacked up outside the mortuary. In a mass grave in Hillside Cemetery, 100 victims were buried, and a memorial marker commemorates this tragic time. Spanish influenza hit Silverton hard, and in just three weeks, 152 people died; that's twelve percent of the population. Silverton lost the greatest percentage of its citizens to Spanish influenza of any other town in the United States.

Hard times lasted until World War II, when many mines resumed operation, producing gold, silver, copper, lead, zinc, tungsten, and manganese. Then in the 1950s, the boom-and-bust cycle returned as many of the larger mines that had survived for years shut down for good. Mining was at a low in Silverton, and the town barely hung on.

Today Silverton's year-round population of 500 is supported by tourism, instead of mining, and the railroad is as important as it was a century ago. Instead of carrying gold and silver from the mines, now 200,000 visitors take the Durango and Silverton Narrow Gauge Railroad to this mining town every year.

Denver & Rio Grande engine on narrow-gauge tracks high above the Animas River. *Courtesy of History Colorado–William Henry Jackson Collection.*

Grand Imperial Hotel

Built by a ladies' corset manufacturer from England, the Grand Hotel opened on July 3, 1883, to a huge celebration. The three-story brick building had been planned for businesses and apartments, but the owner, William Thomson, listened to the local clamor for a fine hotel and converted the third-floor apartments into hotel rooms. There was a large ballroom, and guests enjoyed midnight feasts in the hotel's wood-paneled dining room, illuminated by imported crystal chandeliers. Drinks were served at the saloon's hand-carved, cherry wood bar, with its three French diamond dust mirrors in the matching back bar.

The hotel was across the street from Silverton's oldest bordello-saloon, built in 1875 by Jane Bowman. A London girl, she christened her brothel Westminster Hall and oversaw the construction of a tunnel that ran underneath the street to the hotel.

One of the first shootings at the hotel occurred in July 1885 when a robber broke into the hardware store on the first floor and was killed by the town marshal. There was more gunfire in April 1900 when Jack Turner found out that his lady love, Blanche, a working girl from Blair Street, was having a drink at the saloon with another Jack, a miner named Jack Lambert. He rushed to the Grand and began shooting at the couple seated at the bar, hitting Lambert twice. Blanche was unscathed, but bullets were flying as customers scrambled for cover: one pulled the faro table over on top of himself, another tried to climb a water pipe, a third hid under the poker table, while a fourth crawled under the wine room door and jumped out a window. The sheriff arrested Turner and hauled him off to jail. Lambert recovered from his wounds—and was divorced by his wife.

On September 3, 1904, about 1:00 a.m., a masked man burst through the saloon's front door yelling, "Hands up!" He was waving a pistol and shotgun around when the manager grabbed the gunman's arm, attempting to get his weapon. As the two struggled, the robber fired, striking the manager in the chest and leg. Everyone ducked for cover as the bullets flew. The bartender was hit in the arm, and John Loftus, a young miner standing at the bar, was shot in the abdomen and fell to the floor, mortally wounded. His last words

The Grand Imperial Hotel, opened in 1883, was Silverton's largest building and first fine hotel. *Courtesy of Wendy Williams.*

This antique hand-carved Brunswick bar has a bullet hole, a reminder of numerous shootings in the saloon. *Courtesy of Wendy Williams.*

were, "My God, I'm done for!" The wounded manager staggered out the door and collapsed in the street as the gunman escaped out a back window. The sheriff quickly organized a search, and the murderer was found dead in an alley, a suicide. He was identified as an "honest and trustworthy fellow" who'd accumulated huge gambling debts. The manager and bartender recovered, but John Loftus, just twenty-nine, was buried in Silverton's cemetery.

The saloon was robbed several times as thieves cleaned out the safe and grabbed all the cash from the roulette and faro games. On April 17, 1907, about 3:00 a.m., three masked men strode in the door and commanded, "Throw up your hands!" The robbers were all heavily armed, each with at least one revolver and a sawed-off shotgun. They herded the thirty customers against the wall and swept the money from the gaming tables into ore bags. They emptied out the cash register and went behind the bar where the safe was wide open. Grabbing a money bag containing $1,000 in silver and currency, they raced out the back door with approximately $3,000.

Everyone knew the safe was never locked except the new bartender. When he closed the saloon on his first night, he tossed the money bag in, shut the door, and twirled the dial, locking it tight. The next morning, the safe couldn't be opened because no one knew the combination. This fiasco concluded days later when a safecracker imported from Denver successfully used his skills on the safe.

The hotel weathered several ownership transfers, and the name was changed to the Grand Imperial Hotel in 1909. The robberies continued until the owner finally decided to lock the safe. In 1916, Colorado became a "dry state," four years ahead of national Prohibition, and overnight, the rowdy saloon was transformed into a pool hall, serving soda pop and sarsaparilla. Prohibition hurt the hotel, which closed its restaurant around 1919 and the saloon the following year. During the hard times of the Depression, the mines shut down, and the Miners' Union Hospital closed because it had no money. Then the Grand Imperial Hotel closed.

The hotel's accumulated property taxes were paid in 1921 by Henry Frecker, who was issued a tax deed for the property three years later, according to Colorado law. He leased the hotel to Rosa Stewart, who reopened in 1925 and kept it going by taking boarders. One of Rosa's tenants, fifty-nine-year-old John Zink, became infatuated with her. One day, they had an argument and a furious Zink whipped out his revolver and shot at Rosa point-blank. Luckily, his aim was bad, and he only hit her in the arm and the side. Then he turned the gun on himself, firing one shot into his head. Zink died on the spot, and after Rosa recovered, she left town.

Henry Frecker took over the management and remained at the hotel until his death in February 1944. He willed the hotel to his daughter, Edna Frecker, who was very surprised to learn of her inheritance. Forty years earlier, Frecker had abandoned his family in Victor, Colorado, and disappeared. He was assumed dead. Surprisingly, Frecker had been in Silverton since 1905 and had acquired a mine, which he eventually sold for a large profit. He saved his money and was regarded around town as a tightwad. He bought the Grand Imperial at a bargain price.

Like her father, Edna Frecker wasn't popular, and she was especially disliked by the men of Silverton. She campaigned relentlessly against vice and sin and was determined to close the saloons, dance halls, and brothels. The town fathers breathed a sigh of relief in 1950 when Edna sold the hotel to a wealthy Texan. He went bankrupt after an expensive hotel renovation, and the heating oil supplier found himself the owner of the Grand Imperial as payment of his bill. He sold it to the Broadmoor Hotel of Colorado Springs, who owned it for eighteen years. The hotel has been through several more ownership changes and subsequent renovations.

Ghosts

The hotel's most well-known ghost is Luigi Regalia, a physician who'd come from Italy around 1880. He established a practice and made many friends, but after a failed romance, he sank into gloom and dark despair. On November 1, 1890, Luigi rented room 28, locked his door, and wrote a farewell letter to a friend. Then he picked up his revolver, and holding a small pocket mirror, he put the gun to his head and pulled the trigger. A physician friend and the desk clerk found Luigi lying in a pool of blood, the revolver grasped in his hand. Despite a large hole in his head, Luigi was still breathing. A second physician came, and the two doctors struggled to keep the poor man from dying, but their efforts were futile. About 2:30 a.m. on November 2, 1890, Luigi Regalia breathed his last. He was buried in Hillside Cemetery, mourned by his numerous friends.

Sometime later, a traveling salesman staying at the hotel was awakened by a sound and startled to see a dark figure in a black coat and hat standing near his bed. He described a man with a black, bushy moustache and eyes that were agonized and full of pain. The salesman was terrified, as the shadowy figure slowly approached with his hand outstretched, pleading. He whispered something, and then suddenly he was gone. The salesman jumped out of bed and ran down the stairs to tell the desk clerk. "Oh, you saw Luigi!" she exclaimed and told him the tragic story of Luigi Regalia.

This melancholy spirit is well known around the Grand Imperial, and he has been seen by both guests and employees. He makes his rounds at night, a wispy figure drifting from room to room, and some guests have awakened to see a dark shadow leaning over their bed. One woman said, "I didn't believe in ghosts until I stayed here.…I woke up to a man with a top hat leaning over my bed in the middle of the night. I had no idea this place was haunted until the next morning when I told the staff. They just smiled and said, 'That's Luigi.'"

One former owner told ghost writer Anthony Garcez that Dr. Luigi has often been seen in room 314. Some guests have answered a knock on the door to find a stranger, who introduced himself as a doctor, inquired about their health, then left. Guests have commented on this ghost's life-like appearance and professional demeanor.

There have been several renovations and re-numbering of rooms, so no one is sure where Luigi died. Some employees and guests have seen a strange tableau of a man lying on the bed while a woman in a Victorian dress bends over him. She paces frantically around the room before returning to the bedside as the scene slowly fades away.

This portrait of Lillian Russell in the lobby dates to the hotel's early days. *Courtesy of Wendy Williams.*

Upstairs, doors open and close on their own, startling guests. One man was lying in bed when his room door opened. He went to the door; no one was there, and the hall was empty. He returned to bed, and the door opened again. No one was there. This happened several times, and the man was ready to move to a different room when the activity stopped. Sometimes a flowery fragrance or the scent of spicy men's cologne is noticed in the halls, and many have heard the sound of heavy footsteps. Employees report hearing footsteps approach a guest room where they're working; then the sound stops, and no one is around. Housekeepers complain that they often feel uncomfortable, like they're being watched while they work.

Loud banging is sometimes heard coming from the kitchen at night. The blame is often laid on the spirit of George Foster, who worked in the kitchen and was killed by an avalanche in February 1900. Occasionally a thin, scruffy-looking miner walks up to the saloon's bar and asks for a drink. As the bartender turns to make it, his customer vanishes. A paranormal group, called Haunted Dimensions, spent some time investigating the hotel and identified Luigi's spirit and sixteen other entities. They became aware of various apparitions in the saloon where several people have been killed. The investigators said that this was the most haunted part of the hotel.

The desk clerk said pens and papers are occasionally moved around, and that dragging sounds are heard overhead, like furniture being moved about. This happens after the rooms have been cleaned, when no one is working upstairs. Lights flicker on and off randomly in the halls and rooms, and the updated electrical system can't be responsible. The ghostly figure of a man has been seen in the lobby, where photographers have obtained some unusual photos of orbs and shadowy shapes.

Wyman Hotel

Louis Wyman was thirteen years old when he stowed away on a German ship bound for New York. When the ship docked, he sneaked off and raced down an alley to start a new life with forty-eight cents in his pocket. He could say "yes" and "no" in English and worked at any job he could get. Deciding he'd like to become a cowboy, he headed for the New Mexico Territory in 1874 and was hired as a ranch hand. After about a year, he'd learned a lot about cows, horses, burros, and mules. He'd heard they were shoveling up silver in the streets of Silverton, so he decided to head for Colorado. He owned his horse, and his English was greatly improved.

Wyman was caught in a snowstorm near Raton Pass on the Colorado-New Mexico border and found shelter with "Uncle Dick" Wooten. A mountain man–entrepreneur, Wooten had widened the rugged trail over Raton Pass so trade wagons could pass, and he charged a toll. Louis worked for his room and board at Wooten's ranch until early summer and then left for Colorado.

Louis made it through the mountains to Silverton, where he tried prospecting but did not have any luck and decided to look for other ways to make a living. He worked in a restaurant, hoping to learn to cook, but spent most of his time washing dishes. He earned his U.S. citizenship and changed his last name to "Wyman." He decided he might have a future in the freighting business, hauling supplies to the mines in the mountains. Louis learned how to pack goods on burros and mules as he continued to plan and wash dishes.

Wyman saved his money and bought a small string of burros. They were surefooted on the mountain trails and were much cheaper to feed because they ate the wild grasses and didn't need hay and grain like mules or horses. He contracted to haul mining supplies, food, and equipment to the mines scattered through the San Juan Mountains. Returning from the mines, the burros were loaded with bags of silver ore headed for the smelter. Wyman acquired more pack animals and a wagon, and by 1887, he was operating the largest freighting business in the area. He eventually acquired a building at the edge of Silverton as headquarters for his freighting business and stables for his animals.

The Denver & Rio Grande Railroad had arrived in 1882 and was bringing supplies and equipment from Durango and hauling silver ore to the smelters. The railroad could offer much cheaper rates than Wyman or the other freighters. Some mine owners had built a series of aerial trams using thick wire cables to carry ore in large buckets down from mines perched thousands of feet above. The cables ran in an endless loop and could haul supplies up to the mines. Miners often hitched a ride up or down in the large ore buckets of the tram. One miner described swaying along in an ore bucket as it dropped thousands of feet down a deep canyon as "producing a creepy feeling to the stoutest heart!"

Freight wagons pulled by six-horse teams were still needed to haul the heaviest or largest pieces of equipment, like boilers or compressors, to the mines, but Wyman could see that the freighting business was declining. In 1900, he sold his entire business to the British government. Wyman loaded up his mules, pack saddles, six horse teams and wagons, all the tools, and even spare horseshoes. He took everything east to St. Louis and loaded the animals and goods on barges, and then they floated down the river to New Orleans. There the animals and goods were put on an ocean freighter and taken to South Africa, where they would carry supplies to the British army in the Boer War. Wyman felt some of pangs of regret as he saw his life's work and several four-legged friends, who'd been with him for years, leaving on that freighter.

Returning to Silverton, Wyman tore down his freighting headquarters on Greene Street and built the red sandstone Wyman Building. He carved the images of his favorite pack mules into two large pieces of sandstone and placed them on top of his new building. These monuments to the animals that were so important in his success are still there today.

Silverton needed a community building for the fraternal organizations' meetings, dances and social events. The ladies' clubs, sewing circles, and church groups needed space, too. The new building had a large ballroom, meeting areas, a spacious banquet hall, and a lounge for the ladies. There

Louis Wyman carved the images of his favorite pack mules in the slabs of sandstone displayed on the Wyman Building. *Courtesy of Wendy Williams.*

was indoor plumbing, and the entire first floor was comfortably furnished. Offices on the second floor were rented by doctors, dentists, and mining companies. Several small businesses and the electric light company rented space in the building for years.

In 1911, a friend of Louis's bought an automobile in Denver and wanted to bring it to Silverton, but there were no roads that the car could navigate. The men worked out a plan so Louis's friend and another acquaintance, who was a magazine writer, probably sensing a story, drove the car from Denver to Del Norte. Then they plowed as far as possible up the rough Rio Grande Valley toward the river's headwaters near the beginning of Stony Pass where they met Louis.

The auto, a Croxton-Keeton, was vigorously cranked until it sputtered, then caught, started, and settled into a reassuring rumble. Off they went. The car got across the shallow Rio Grande River and then began the steep climb up the mountain. They struggled along in deep ruts, avoiding rocks and trying to protect the undercarriage. They blew out a tire, and after finally getting it changed, the men used a hand pump to inflate it with ninety pounds of air pressure. Exhausted, they crossed the Rio Grande thirteen more times, trying to avoid the river's numerous boulders. These crossings would not have been a problem for a pack train, but after each crossing, the car crawled out of the river like a tired old turtle. As they slowly approached the summit of Stony Pass, creeping around sharp switchbacks, the tires squealed over slippery rocks as the radiator sent up jets of steam. The car was chuffing and coughing, and the carburetor barely functioned at twelve thousand feet in altitude.

The car clawed its way up the last steep grade and groaned to a stop a short distance from the top. The wheezing machine could go no further, so it was chained to a team of huge dapple grays that Wyman had arranged to have waiting nearby—just in case. The team had no trouble pulling the car over 12,500-foot-high Stony Pass. The writer snapped plenty of photos before they started downhill toward Silverton. The car's tendency to hurtle forward like a rocket frightened everyone, and they had to stop often to cool the brakes before lurching forward again. They breathed much easier when they finally skidded around the last curve to level ground. When they drove triumphantly into town, they were greeted by a cheering crowd waving American flags, while the fire bell rang wildly. The Silverton Brass Band struck up a rousing Sousa march, and blasts of dynamite were set off from a hillside. The writer described the journey vividly in *Outdoor Life* magazine, and the folks in Silverton got their first look at an automobile.

The Depression brought hard times to Silverton, and as businesses failed, the Wyman Building lost its tenants. Louis remodeled the first floor to accommodate a meat market and dry goods store, but both businesses failed. Then he developed cancer in an old leg injury and died in 1924. His casket was placed on a mule-drawn sled for the short journey to Hillside Cemetery, where his many friends and business acquaintances gathered for his burial.

David Wyman, Louis's brother, paid the taxes on the building and sold it to a friend. The first floor was converted into a warm winter garage with storage for miners working at the Mayflower Mine and Mill. This arrangement collapsed when the mine and mill closed, leaving the miners without jobs. The building went through several ownership changes and was eventually remodeled and converted into a hotel. Now this building has been included in the National Register of Historic Places.

Ghosts

Guests and employees complain about misplaced personal items, mysterious sounds, and shadowy figures in this old building, Employees have help making beds, straightening rooms and cleaning, and some say Mrs. Wyman's spirit is making sure the hotel runs smoothly.

The shadowy shape of a woman has been seen in the upstairs hall, and she's usually carrying a bundle of towels or sheets. A previous owner told

The Wyman trolley picks up passengers at the railroad depot and brings them to the hotel. *Courtesy of Wendy Williams.*

an investigator that she sometimes felt like she was being watched when she was working at the front desk. She thought this was a helpful presence and recalled instances when items and papers she'd been looking for would suddenly turn up in unusual places. The owner recalled times when she needed help with a difficult task, and miraculously, she'd suddenly get it done, "As if I had someone helping me!"

10
OURAY

On Christmas Day 1875, a little group of prospectors feasted on wild turkey and toasted their good fortune with a big shot of—vinegar. They had no wine or whiskey, so they decided that vinegar was the next best thing. These prospectors really had a lot to be happy about because they'd all found deposits of gold or silver and were busily working their claims. In the summer of 1875, they'd struggled over Engineer Mountain north of Silverton and trudged down the steep slopes into a small valley that was surrounded on three sides by sheer cliffs and towering mountains. Prospectors Gus Begole and John Eckles hadn't had much luck in Silverton, but it changed in the valley. They were first to discover two small gold deposits, which they named the Cedar and the Clipper. Two other prospectors, who had been fishing, discovered the Trout and Fisherman lodes.

Begole and Eckles continued prospecting in the valley, and in October 1875, they made an extremely rich find they called the Mineral Farm. This claim had parallel veins of gold ore that ran along so close to the surface that they could mine it just like digging potatoes. Several rich silver lodes were found in the high mountains above the camp, including the Virginius, at an altitude of 12,500 feet. This group of silver mines at 11,000 to 12,000 feet became one of the most valuable mining districts in the San Juan Mountains.

A prospector, Andy Richardson, traveled over a high pass, which he named Imogene after his wife, and reached an alpine basin where he made several gold discoveries. Others crossed from the Red Mountain area and tramped further westward to another alpine valley, which they named Yankee Boy

Basin. There the Wright brothers discovered a vein of gold that was eighteen to twenty inches wide and even contained a large amount of silver. It became the fabulously rich Wheel of Fortune Mine A townsite was laid out in the valley and named for "Uncompahgre City," the Ute word for "warm springs."

The hot springs at the north end of the valley had been used by the Indians for centuries, and they continued their soaks with the prospectors. These Utes and their leader, Ouray, were friendly and often visited the new settlement to trade. They were skilled horsemen and were always ready for a horse race. The Utes bet heavily on their favorites, which usually won.

During the first winter of 1875–76, the few prospectors who remained in the camp ran out of food and supplies, and by spring, everyone was near starvation. Thankfully, spring came early in 1876, and the first men who managed to get through the deep snow were welcomed with joyful shouts. A merchant named Randall brought a stock of dry goods and groceries and started a store in the camp's first log cabin. Two others began a mercantile business in a tent with a cracker box for a counter and an old sheet-iron stove as their safe. James and Mary Dixon opened the first hotel in their own log cabin. Their guests slept on the floor and provided their own blankets. The first saloon opened, followed by a meat market and a blacksmith shop.

The camp's name was changed to "Ouray" for the Ute leader, and by the end of 1876, the population was 400. There were 214 cabins and tents, 4 general stores, a sawmill, an ore sampling works, 2 hotels, and a school with 43 students. Soon there were 7 saloons, several gambling dens, and a brothel. When prospectors came into town on weekends, the population swelled to more than 1,000.

On Christmas 1876, everyone was invited to a huge celebration. The ladies cooked a splendid holiday feast, which they served on long tables in the butcher shop. There were plenty of toasts—with traditional spirits—and dancing that lasted into the early hours of the morning. The winter of 1876–77 was severe, and game was scarce. There was no meat for weeks, which made old bacon rinds and dried apples a real treat. Despite rationing, the prospectors ran out of food again and survived on bread and coffee. This second hungry winter taught the town's merchants to stock up on enormous amounts of food and supplies in the fall so there would be enough to last until the spring snows melted. Food was hauled into the mountains in wagons as far as possible and then loaded on pack trains and taken to remote camps. In the winter, when the snow in the passes reached depths of twenty to thirty feet, all travel stopped, isolating the camps as their meager food supplies dwindled.

In 1876, Colorado became the thirty-eighth state in the Union, and the following January the legislature created Ouray County and named Ouray the county seat. Ouray's newspaper, the *Solid Muldoon*, first published in 1879, was an instant success, and readers loved the sharp, sarcastic wit of its editor, Dave Day. He was interested in politics and often ridiculed pompous politicians and devious mine promoters in the paper. The *Solid Muldoon* was read far and wide, and Day's humorous, scathing observations were often quoted.

In 1881, Otto Mears began work on a toll road south from Ouray through the rugged mountains to the booming mining camps on Red Mountain. Previous attempts to construct a road had failed. Mears had no special training, and his knowledge was based solely on his experience building toll roads throughout the San Juans. He decided that most of the road would have to be blasted through rock cliffs, creating a shelf road above the Animas River. Men were lowered down the high cliffs on ropes to drill holes, place dynamite, then light the fuses. Their lives depended upon how fast their fellow workers could pull them back up before the dynamite exploded. Five men were killed working on this hazardous section. After months of blasting, Mears succeeded in constructing a narrow, precipitous trail through the gorge more than five hundred feet above the river.

When the road was completed, only the bravest ventured over it to reach the silver-rich Red Mountain camps. Next, Mears and his brave crew set to work gradually widening the trail so a mule-drawn wagon could creep around its sharp curves. He put a toll gate at Bear Creek Falls and built a small cabin for the gate tender, and then he constructed a bridge across a wide chasm and wide waterfall. The road construction cost nearly $100,000 in 1883 money, and in those days, there were no federal funds to help. Otto Mears often said this was the most difficult project he'd ever undertaken. The completion of these few miles of road was considered one of the greatest feats of engineering and road construction in this nation. Mears extended the road from Red Mountain to Silverton in 1884.

In December 1887, everyone in Ouray gathered to cheer the Denver & Rio Grande train when it chugged into the Ouray depot. The completion of an extension line from Montrose meant that passengers who'd been careening and bouncing about on stagecoaches now could ride in comfort in a passenger car pulled by a steam locomotive. The railroad was a cheaper way to ship vegetables, fruit, and ore, and it put the freight wagons and pack trains out of business.

The 1893 repeal of the Sherman Silver Purchase Act was devastating to Ouray, causing businesses to fail and banks to collapse. The city turned

The Ouray to Silverton Toll Road, narrow and treacherous, was blasted through solid rock cliffs. *Courtesy of History Colorado–William Henry Jackson Collection.*

The Wright's Opera House has an ornate cast-iron front that was believed to make it fireproof. *Courtesy of Wendy Williams.*

off the electric street lights and laid off its employees. In 1896, Thomas Walsh, a carpenter who'd been prospecting for years and studying mining technology at night, discovered high-grade gold ore in the discarded rocks from two abandoned silver mines in Imogene Basin. He bought these old silver claims, combined them, and named his new gold mine Camp Bird, after the area's noisy gray jays. Then he hired five hundred miners for a high wage, began mining gold and built a large stamp mill, which processed two hundred tons of ore a day.

 The Camp Bird boardinghouse at 11,200 feet altitude accommodated four hundred men and had a game-club room with billiards and poolroom, and a reading room where the miners could spend their off-hours listening to the phonograph or reading newspapers, magazines, and books. The building had electricity, steam heat, hot and cold running water, porcelain bath tubs, and marble-topped vanities with sinks and flush toilets. Good food was served on china dishes by well-dressed waiters as soft music played in the background.

 Despite his rapidly accumulating wealth, Tom Walsh remained down-to-earth and was well liked by the people of Ouray. He and his family lived in town, and everyone was always invited to the Walsh parties and dances. He built a public library for Ouray's citizens, supplied it with over six thousand books, and set up a fund to buy more books annually. The library dedication on July 24, 1901, was a gala affair attended by the governor of Colorado, the former governor, mayors, and dignitaries. Walsh published an apology to Ouray's citizens in the newspaper, expressing regret that lack of space prevented him from inviting everyone.

From 1896 to 1902, the Camp Bird Mine produced about $4 million in gold per year; that's about $5,000 per day, making Walsh a multimillionaire. Unfortunately, he developed health problems that were aggravated by Ouray's high altitude and cold winters and decided to sell the mine. Walsh moved his family to Washington, D.C., and, as a partner with King Leopold of Belgium, opened new gold mines in the Congo. Tom Walsh died suddenly in 1909, but his Camp Bird Mine continued to operate, and by 1916, it had produced over $27 million in gold. His daughter, Evalyn, married Edward McLean, a newspaper heir, and purchased the huge Hope Diamond. Considered the world's most perfect blue diamond, it's now in the Smithsonian.

Ouray's good old days ended officially in 1916 when voters approved Prohibition. People in the San Juans voted against the liquor ban but were

The large warm springs pool opened in the 1920s and draws crowds today. *Courtesy of Wendy Williams.*

overruled by the rest of Colorado's population. Enterprising citizens became bootleggers and hid their stills in old mine tunnels, abandoned buildings, and even in fine Victorian homes.

Ouray's many hot springs bubbling up along the Uncompahgre River from underground fissures have been a natural draw for weary, aching people for centuries. In 1920, local citizens bought pool memberships, and businesses contributed funds to build a large outdoor pool around the hot springs. The pool opened on July 4, 1927, and a huge crowd came to swim and soak in the water, which was believed to be helpful in curing arthritis and other ailments.

In 1916, federal funds provided by the Good Roads bill, combined with modern road engineering techniques, were used to improve the narrow, rugged wagon road built by Otto Mears into one that could be safely used by automobiles. In 1924, this shelf road became part of the Million Dollar Highway when it opened to cars. The new road brought tourists to Ouray, where they raved about the beauty of its waterfalls and the surrounding mountains. In 1935, Ouray received a WPA grant that put unemployed men to work, making more safety improvements on this highway.

Most of the core of Ouray's business district and its commercial buildings date from 1876 to 1915. The houses vary from plain log cabins, built around 1875, to many homes in a variety of Victorian and Italianate architectural styles. Much of the town was designated as a National Historic District in 2006.

Beaumont Hotel

For more than thirty years, the elegant Beaumont Hotel, once the showplace of Ouray, sat neglected, the shabby symbol of an old grudge. Its wealthy owner, Wayland Phillips, furious after a dispute with the city government in 1967, closed the hotel and swore, "It'll never open in my lifetime!" Then she had the windows boarded up, the doors nailed shut and, as a final insult, she painted the hotel bright pink.

The Beaumont, known as "The Queen of the San Juans," was a sorry sight, bedraggled and down at the heels. Mice scurried through the grand ballroom where bejeweled ladies and gentlemen had danced the night away. The crystal chandeliers, once festooned with flowers, were draped in spidery cobwebs. Water dripped on the fine furniture through holes in the roof, and the oak floors creaked and groaned as snow piled up in the corners. Expensive hand-painted wallpaper drooped and molded. Cold drafts stirred the gauzy lace curtains, which flapped at the windows like ghosts waving hello. As the years passed, the hotel became more run-down, and there was even talk of blowing it up. Then in 1998, Wayland Phillips died, and the hotel was sold at auction to Dan and Mary King for $850,000.

In 1886, the construction of a "really fine hotel" was financed by five businessmen who decided Ouray needed a place where wealthy investors and entrepreneurs could stay while conducting their affairs. The three-story hotel was one of the first buildings in town to have electricity and cold running water. Hot water was piped in from the nearby springs. The hotel was built of brick, and it had a Gothic tower that was two stories higher than the rest of the building. The financiers believed the tower, topped by a golden weather vane, gave the building more class. Like many hotels built during this period, the Beaumont had two front entrances: one on Fifth Avenue for the ladies, while the gentlemen entered from Third Street.

The Beaumont, the "Flagship of the San Juans," was painted pink and closed for thirty years by its owner. *Courtesy of Wendy Williams.*

The lobby-atrium's gold velour wallpaper gleamed, and a large skylight bathed the entire area in wonderful light. There were two banks on the first floor, the Western Union Telegraph office, and a gentlemen's barbershop. An impressive golden oak staircase led to the upper floors, which had forty-three guest rooms with baths. They were furnished with the finest from Marshall Fields of Chicago. There were interior balconies on the second and third floors, circling the central atrium, which opened to the skylight and gave guests a bird's-eye view of the lobby below.

The grand opening was held July 7, 1887, and the Palmer House in Chicago sent its most experienced employees to help with the gala affair. The distinguished guests included King Leopold of Belgium, Teddy Roosevelt, and Herbert Hoover, then a young mining engineer. Sarah Bernhardt and Lillie Langtry entertained wealthy investors and mining millionaires in the ballroom. Ouray's newspaper, the *Solid Muldoon*, raved, "The ballroom was crowded with dancers until daylight.…[T]he hungry did justice to the bounteous spread."

Both the Beaumont and the Western Hotel sent carriages daily to meet travelers arriving at the train depot. To attract more guests, each driver would loudly shout out his hotel's wonderful accommodations and special features. As they acquired additional guests, each was seated in the buggy with a flourish, their luggage loaded up, and the driver drove off triumphantly. The elegant Wright Opera House was built across the street from the Beaumont in 1888, and guests could stroll across the street for the evening performance.

By 1896, Thomas Walsh owned many of the old silver mines around Ouray and was mining their waste dumps for gold. The Camp Bird gold mine was flourishing, and on December 10, 1896, Walsh hosted a ball at the Beaumont for over one hundred guests that was described in the *Ouray Herald*. Bouquets of beautiful cut flowers came from Denver on the train, and the ballroom had "massive banks of pink and white chrysanthemums and carnations. Various colored globes were supplied to the lights, throwing a soft, mellow glow over the many fair dancers who tripped the light fantastic until the early hours." The journalist continued, "The gentlemen were attired in the faultless conventional evening dress, while the ladies were perfection in attire composed of rich fabrics and adorned in profusion with brilliant diamonds and other precious stones; all presenting a scene of rare beauty."

In 1911, Chipeta, the popular widow of Ouray, the respected chief of the Utes, and her family visited the town and stayed at the Beaumont. A

Passengers arrived regularly on the stagecoach to enjoy the luxury of the Beaumont Hotel. *Courtesy of History Colorado.*

special committee directed the festivities, and many photographs were taken of her visit. A concert was given in Chipeta's honor in the evening by the town's band, and the city fathers took her for a ride in one of the first automobiles in Ouray. This car was also the first to make the journey over Otto Mears's rugged road from Red Mountain to Ouray. The coughs, belches, and backfires of this mechanical marvel terrified horses, sending them into snorting, bucking fits. Often a horseback rider went ahead of an approaching auto to warn the drivers of wagons and buggies that a horseless machine was coming.

Walsh's Camp Bird gold mine helped Ouray survive the depression of 1893, but production slowed during World War I. The Great Depression following the 1929 stock market crash brought massive unemployment, business and bank failures. The Beaumont closed many rooms and put furniture in storage, hoping for better days. The hotel was sold in 1941 and fell into Wayland Phillip's hands in 1967. Then the silly dispute over her parking space caused the closure of the hotel for thirty years.

In 1998, after the death of Mrs. Phillips, the hotel was purchased at auction by Dan and Mary King. The people of Ouray were excited by the prospect of new owners, who were interested in rehabilitating the hotel and eventually reopening it. Older people reminisced about having Sunday dinner in the dining room and recalled special celebrations that had been held at the Beaumont. Families celebrated birthdays, anniversaries, weddings and special occasions here, and the hotel held a special place in the community's heart. Dan King remarked, "The people are so in love with this building, both the city and its people feel like they own it."

The Kings began restoration work in the early 2000s, and their first project was the removal of the peeling, pink paint, a laborious process that took five months. The bricks were heated with small propane torches, which caused the paint to bubble. Then it was scraped off, and the bricks were scrubbed vigorously with brushes. The deteriorated bricks and mortar were replaced, and all were restored to their natural color.

Another huge task was restoring the eight different types of handmade windows. They were all removed, repaired, and returned to their original locations. This was a much more expensive project than simply buying new windows. The floors were leveled, repaired or replaced, and the interior walls and roof were stabilized with twelve tons of steel. The plumbing, heating, and electrical wiring were updated, and the building was brought up to code while maintaining its historical appearance.

The wallpaper was especially challenging because there were as many as twelve different layers of paper under the moldy top one. In the lobby, seventeen layers covered the original 1886 wallpaper. Surprisingly, the company that designed this paper a century earlier was still in business and was able to make an exact replica of the original.

The old clock on the staircase landing had been ruined when the hotel was closed, and its repair was questionable. Research showed that this clock was one of only eight that had been made in the 1880s by a clockmaker in New York. The Beaumont's clock was the original Number Eight, and it needed parts. Experts tracked down enough pieces of the original Clock Number Four on eBay to repair Number Eight. Today, the clock that visitors see quietly ticking away is a combination of the parts of two 130-year-old time pieces.

The Beaumont's grand opening was October 7, 2002, after a $6 million renovation and restoration. In the lobby, the original registration desk, the tall walk-in safe, and the Chickering grand piano date to 1886. The Tundra Restaurant on the second floor gleams with its original wood paneling and

A skylight illuminates the Beaumont's lobby, the original front desk, and tall antique safe. *Courtesy of Wendy Williams.*

The antique clock displayed on the landing is one of only eight made in the 1880s. *Courtesy of Wendy Williams.*

rosewood trim, while upstairs, each guest room has at least one refurbished piece of the hotel's original furniture. The renovation of the Beaumont earned the Colorado Governor's Award for Historic Preservation and one of only four Preserve America Presidential Awards. In the National Register of Historic Places, the Beaumont gleams and shines with its old elegance and now boasts a luxurious spa. Once again, this lovely boutique hotel deserves its name, "The Flagship of the San Juans."

Ghosts

The Beaumont is haunted by the spirit of Ellar Day, a nineteen-year-old waitress hired for the 1886 opening. Born in Ouray, she was supporting her young son and was well liked at the hotel. Problems developed when the black pastry chef, Joseph Dixon, became infatuated with Ellar and pursued her relentlessly. When she spurned his advances, the chef became angry and threatening. On September 13, 1887, Dixon, furious and drunk, burst into Ellar's third-floor room and shot her several times. Ellar's father, the hotel plumber, trying to protect her, hit Dixon in the head with a heavy pitcher. When his gun was empty, the chef staggered down the back stairs into the arms of the sheriff, who hauled him off to jail. Friends found Mr. Day covered in blood, cradling his dying daughter in his arms.

The *Solid Muldoon* reported that the chef had been fired by several hotels because of his "wicked temperament," adding that he'd threatened to kill others. The citizens of Ouray were outraged, and the town's mood grew ugly. When night fell, an angry mob of masked citizens came to the jail, demanding the keys, but they were turned back by the sheriff. The crowd eventually dispersed, and the town grew quiet. Hours later, an alarm sounded as bright flames sprang up from all corners of the jail. The building burned quickly, and when the flames were finally subdued, the sheriff found Joe Dixon dead in his cell, overcome by the dense smoke. Everyone in town knew the mob had set the jail on fire.

Soon after the tragedy, quiet nights at the Beaumont were shattered by unearthly screams, and blood spatters appeared on the wall in Ellar's room. Shadowy specters were seen slipping down the back stairs and around corners. In 1896, Alexander Blake, a hotel guest, was awakened by gunshots and threw his door open to see a "blood-drenched girl" running down the hall. Blake followed her and stumbled into the night clerk, who assured him that no one had been shot. Frantically, Blake insisted he'd seen a bleeding girl, despite being told repeatedly, "It's a ghost—only a ghost!"

Another guest sensed a frightening presence in her room, which was especially strong near the window draperies. When she cautiously peeked behind them, she saw nothing. She said that she was really scared in the bathroom and insisted that something was in there with her.

During the years that the hotel was boarded up with dust, gloom and ghosts, passersby reported hearing faint screams and an occasional pop like a gunshot inside the building. A psychic, who visited Ouray before the renovations, said she heard music and laughter coming from the building, and she noticed the clip-clop of horses' hooves and the sound of carriage wheels.

When author Anthony Garcez visited the Beaumont, he was drawn to the Buckskin Bookstore on the first floor of the hotel. He interviewed the owner, who said she often heard footsteps in the store when she was alone. There was an occasional banging and knocking in the rear of the building when no one was around. Books flew off the shelves and slammed onto the floor when they hadn't been touched by human hands. She recalled that three books flew from nearby shelves and landed neatly at the cash register near two customers. She believed the ghosts in the building wanted to make their presence known. She said that she often felt like she was being watched and even whirled around to find she was alone. Other employees reported similar experiences.

St. Elmo Hotel

Young Kitty O'Brien Porter came to Ouray about 1886 with her twelve-year-old son, Freddie. She landed a job managing the Bon Ton Restaurant, worked hard and eventually saved enough money to buy the restaurant. Kitty's day began about 5:00 a.m. and ran until midnight, seven days a week. She cooked meals, waited on tables, washed stacks of dirty dishes and, at the end of the day, tackled the bills. Kitty's hard work paid off, and her restaurant was popular in Ouray. The *Solid Muldoon* expressed the local sentiment: "The Bon Ton combines excellent fare and courteous treatment to a degree that renders living kind of home-like. It is by far the best establishment in Ouray."

Kitty was quite attractive and had plenty of suitors. She married an electrician, Joseph Heit, on April 30, 1889, and within a few years, the couple adopted a young boy named Francis. When the silver mines closed in 1893, hundreds of miners lost their jobs and were broke, and down on their luck, but they could always get a free meal at the Bon Ton. Kitty never turned anyone away. She survived the economic depression, continued to work hard and saved money.

By 1897, Kitty had enough cash to start construction on a hotel next door to her restaurant. It was completed the following spring, and she named the hotel the St. Elmo. It had arched stained-glass windows with a large second-floor bay window that looked out on Main Street. The rooms had marble-top armoires, brass or mahogany beds, and bright flowery wallpaper. This was an affordable "miners' hotel," and the April 21, 1898 *Ouray Herald* advertised its rates for "regular boarders $1.00 per day: transients $1.50 and new and modern in all its appointments." Meals were available next door at the Bon Ton Restaurant. Kitty was well liked in Ouray and was everyone's friend, always ready to extend a helping hand to anyone in need.

Hardworking Kitty Heit's dream was realized with the opening of the St. Elmo Hotel on Main Street. *Courtesy of Wendy Williams.*

In 1909, fire destroyed many of Ouray's wooden frame buildings, but the St. Elmo and the Bon Ton escaped the flames. In the fall, a heavy cloudburst sent gallons of water, mud and boulders roaring through town, washing out bridges and roads, and sweeping away buildings. Again, Kitty's establishments weren't damaged.

When labor trouble began in the 1900s, Kitty was sympathetic to the union movement. The hotel and restaurant were popular places for Miners' Union meetings and social events. When striking members of the Western Federation of Labor were deported from Telluride, Kitty took many into her hotel until they could return to their homes. She took care of miners injured during the turmoil and assisted their families. "Aunt Kitty" was beloved and respected by the miners and their families.

The citizens of Ouray were shocked in 1915 when they learned that Kitty Heit had suffered a sudden massive heart attack and died at age sixty-six. She was mourned by many, and the *Ouray Herald* described her as "the miner's friend" and paid her tribute:

> *Her many acts of kindness and charity are legion and she was recognized as the miners' friend. They were always welcome at her home whether flush with money or down and out. Her hotel came about as near being a real home for the lonesome and homeless as possible and everything was done for the comfort and pleasure of "her boys." During her residence in Ouray, she had been a regular "mother" to hundreds and no one could possibly be missed more than she.*

Kitty's son, Freddie, took over the hotel, but he lacked his mother's determination and dedication. Kitty had been discouraged by his laziness and lack of interest in the business, and Freddie did a poor job after her death. Kitty's second son, Francis, had enlisted in the military and was off to World War I before she died. He immediately headed home upon learning of his mother's death and was disgusted at the sorry state of her business affairs. Freddie had frittered away everything his mother had worked so hard for. He'd wasted so much money drinking and gambling that her beloved St. Elmo Hotel was on the auction block. When it was sold, the cash went to pay Freddie's gambling debts.

Broke and depressed, Freddie continued to drink while Ouray's citizens didn't hesitate to show their disappointment and scorn. Freddie had few friends left, sank into despair and committed suicide by shooting himself. After Freddie's death, his wife regained control of the hotel and transferred

The bell at the front desk of the St. Elmo often rings mysteriously when no one's there. *Courtesy of Wendy Williams.*

its ownership to Francis in 1920. He built up the business once again and operated the hotel successfully for three years before selling it.

Through the years, the St. Elmo Hotel changed hands several times and has been restored to its original appearance. Stucco that was slapped over the brick exterior has been removed, a new bay window has been installed above the entrance, and the hotel has been returned to its former Victorian style with antiques and period-style wallpaper.

The parlor's French doors open onto a patio where the original Bon Ton Restaurant once served Ouray's citizens. That building was torn down in 1924, and the present Bon Ton Restaurant reopened in 1977 on the hotel's lower level. The old rock walls, hardwood floors, warm lighting, and beautiful polished mahogany bar enhance its charm. Today's Bon Ton is regarded as one of the best restaurants on the Western Slope. The St. Elmo Hotel is included in the Ouray National Historic District.

Ghosts

The St. Elmo has several protective spirits hovering about the premises, paying close attention to its operation. Most paranormal experts believe that Freddie is watching over the hotel that he neglected so badly during his lifetime. Francis was always the responsible son, and some people believe that he, too, is keeping a sharp eye on the hotel—and his brother.

A medium, who was drawn to the St. Elmo on visits to Ouray, said she sensed the spirit of Francis and another man in the hotel. She felt that Francis was very angry because Freddie had lost the hotel and said she believed there had been a fierce argument between the brothers. She even speculated that Francis might have shot Freddie. There is no proof to back up this theory, and most people believe that Freddie took his own life.

Sometimes the St. Elmo's protective spirits make their presence known by ringing the bell at the front desk. Employees hurry to the lobby, thinking a guest has arrived, but no one is there. They return to their tasks, and then the bell rings again. Sometimes the ringing is ignored, while a live guest waits—and waits.

Western Hotel

The Western Hotel, built in 1891, has survived the ravages of time, and it is in the National Register of Historic Places and is included in the Ouray National Historic District. Conveniently near the "red-light" district, a tunnel went to one of the popular bordellos and was an ideal place to conceal liquor during Prohibition.

When the Western opened in 1892, it was advertised as "the miners' hotel with forty-three sleeping rooms, three toilets, and a bath tub." Some called it a "miners' palace" with its inviting lobby, richly paneled woodwork, stained-glass windows, electric lights, and fine Victorian furniture. The comfortable sleeping rooms rented for $1.25 a night, and a meal was included for an additional $0.25. The dining room was known for its delicious food, and many townspeople ate there instead of at Ouray's more expensive restaurants. The saloon was a popular place where hotel guests, miners, and local citizens relaxed with a drink and cigar.

The Western was one of Ouray's finest hotels and more affordable than the Beaumont, which charged three to four dollars a night. In 1896, the

Left: Built in 1891, the Western Hotel is the largest wood frame building of its era still standing in Colorado. *Courtesy of Wendy Williams.*

Below: The lobby of the Western Hotel looks much as it did a century ago. *Courtesy of Wendy Williams.*

Ouray Plaindealer called it "an authentic hotel of the Old West." It was sold in 1899, and in 1916, Floro and Maria Flor purchased it. They welcomed travelers, but many of their rooms were rented to miners, who were permanent boarders. Maria took care of the men when they were sick, saw that their laundry was done, helped them write letters and was affectionately called "Mother Flor." Even though a miner was down on his luck, he was always welcome at the Western.

The Flors raised seven children at the hotel and managed to keep it open during the Depression. After Floro died in 1936, Maria carried on the business alone. When the years began to catch up with her, Mother Flor leased the hotel but retained ownership. In 1961, when she was eighty years old, she decided to sell her beloved hotel. Born in 1875, she'd seen many changes: the discovery of silver in Ouray, the growth of the town, the Depression, and two world wars. Mother Flor died in 1963 and was buried in Cedar Hill Cemetery beside her husband.

The Western's lobby, with its high tin ceiling, creaky hardwood floors, and Victorian furnishings, hasn't changed much since the 1890s. The adjacent saloon, with its original carved wooden bar, potbellied stove, spittoons, and mounted trophies is an echo of the past. Visitors are intrigued by the portrait of a woman painted on the floor, which is similar to *The Face on the Barroom Floor* in the Teller House in Central City. Both portraits are the work of artist Herndon Davis, and the mysterious face belongs to his wife, Juanita.

There are fourteen guest rooms on the second floor, with two that have private baths. Room no. 1 has its original marble sink and hand-painted, blue wallpaper. There have been few changes in these old rooms, and they look like they did one hundred years ago. There are about twenty more rooms on the third floor that are not in use. What the Western lacks in amenities, it makes up in authenticity and character. One visitor summed it up, "Walk into the Western, and you walk into the past."

The Face on the Bar Room Floor is the work of artist Herndon Davis. *Courtesy of Wendy Williams.*

Ghosts

John Hopkins, a young miner, who committed suicide here, did not find peace when he died, and his restless spirit wanders about at night. In 1902, the Silverton mine where he worked shut down, and he was unable to find another job. Hopkins's loss of income was overshadowed by the recent death of his beloved wife, and grief transformed him from a pleasant fellow into a gaunt, gloomy shadow. He was drowning in sorrow. On December 27, 1902, Hopkins wrote a letter to his former landlady in Silverton. Next, he composed a farewell letter to his mother and asked her forgiveness. Then he undressed, put his folded clothes on a chair, and crawled into bed.

When Hopkins didn't appear at mealtime for a couple of days, the manager went upstairs to his room and was horrified to find the young man dead. An empty poison bottle lay on the floor, and there was a stack of letters on the desk. The first asked that the letters be mailed and continued, "An inquest will not be necessary. I take my own life—being tired of life and unable to get work, I take this way out of my troubles." John Hopkins was only twenty-one years old when he was laid to rest in the Hillside Cemetery in Silverton.

Now his spirit, full of remorse and sadness, lingers in the hotel. Sudden cold drafts blow through the narrow hall upstairs, and footsteps are heard when no one's around. Employees and guests have been frightened by a partial or full apparition of a man that most believe is Hopkins. Some say this entity looks life-like, except for a gray pallor, and a horrible grimace on his face. "He looks like he's in pain," shuddered one lady who awoke to see the ghost standing at her bedside.

A guest noticed a stack of clothing on a chair when she first entered her room, but she didn't think much about it, Later, the clothes were gone. During the night, she was awakened by a cold chill in the room and was terrified to see a filmy figure standing nearby, gazing at her. She said it was "holding out his hands as if he was begging for help." She said the figure had a "a pleading expression," and she was so frightened that she just pulled the covers over her head. She lay there, frozen with fear, and when she found the courage to peek out, he was gone.

The misty apparition of a plump woman is occasionally seen on the stairs to the second floor, and a little girl has been glimpsed here, too. Another guest woke up to see a young girl standing near her bed. She was wearing a white, gauzy petticoat and one stocking, and her long, reddish blonde hair was ruffled by a breeze coming through the open window. As the frightened

The bar of the Western Hotel has been a popular place for more than one hundred years. *Courtesy of Wendy Williams.*

guest watched, the little figure slowly faded away. When she told the owners about her unusual visitor, they shared the story of a previous owner whose young daughter had perished in a snowstorm.

Two guests in room 18 awoke early one morning to see a woman's hat floating along the ceiling. When it suddenly fell to the floor, the ceiling light fixture began to gyrate wildly. Then a decanter tumbled off the dresser as if it had been swept aside by an invisible hand. When the activity finally ceased, the frightened couple tried to grab a few winks but were awaked by the bed shaking and bouncing about. The man became very upset and yelled, "For Heaven's sake, please stop!" The shaking stopped immediately.

Plenty of unusual encounters and scary experiences are recorded by guests in the journals in each room.

11
TELLURIDE

On June 24, 1889, Butch Cassidy launched his outlaw career by robbing the San Miguel Valley Bank in Telluride. He and two other cowboys held the tellers at gunpoint, grabbed the cash, about $24,000, and dashed out of town, hooting and hollering. The sheriff quickly formed a posse and followed their trail into the mountains, but they eluded the lawmen and dropped out of sight.

The bank was doing well when it was robbed, and Telluride was flush with the profits of the booming gold and silver mines in the surrounding mountains. The first gold strike had been made in 1875 by John Fallon in a high alpine valley. He named his claim the Sheridan and went on to find three more deep lodes (veins) of gold, which he recorded as the Sheridan group in October 1875.

The Smuggler claim was squeezed in next to the Sheridan on the widest, richest, deepest part of the gold vein, and these claims produced millions of dollars. Prospectors rushed to the high alpine basins surrounded by towering peaks, which rise almost perpendicular above the horseshoe-shaped valley. Here, they found spectacular silver and gold deposits in the alpine basins.

In October 1877, San Miguel was the first settlement in the valley, and two miles east, a second town called Columbia was incorporated by the unanimous decision of its twenty-eight voters. Closer to the mines, Columbia quickly outgrew San Miguel to boast a population of two hundred men and five women. They were becoming frustrated because their mail was going to Columbia, California, in the Gold Country. When they proposed

Left: The Mahr Building once housed the bank held up by Butch Cassidy in 1889. *Courtesy of Wendy Williams.*

Below: The white building (*second from the left*) once housed the San Miguel Bank, robbed by Butch Cassidy. *Courtesy of Wendy Williams.*

the new name of "Telluride," for their town, postal officials refused to authorize it. The mail continued to go to California until 1878 when the post office finally accepted the new name and authorized a post office for Telluride, Colorado. This name came from the element tellurium, which forms telluride compounds with gold and silver. Although it was not found in the mountains around Telluride, it is associated with deposits of these rich minerals. Another popular story of how the town got its name is linked to the contraction of "To Hell You Ride," the phrase often yelled at a hopeful prospector setting out for this remote area.

Telluride's main street, Colorado Avenue, was wide enough for long pack trains to turn around, but despite the wealth of its mines, Telluride's growth was slow because of its isolation. In 1881, Otto Mears built the Dallas and San Miguel Toll Road, which ran from the town of Dallas, west of the San Juan Range, for twenty-seven miles, skirting the mountains to reach Telluride. Wagons could travel on this road, which helped decrease the cost of transporting ore out of the valley. As more merchants and tradesmen set up new businesses, the population grew. By 1881, corner business lots were selling for twenty-five dollars, and residence lots went for seventy-five cents. Before long, nearly one thousand people were patronizing Telluride's thirteen saloons and two grocery stores. Water was hauled from the San Miguel River and delivered to homes, saloons, and businesses for ten cents for five gallons.

In 1883, it became the county seat of the new San Miguel County. Many of the richest mines were located in the alpine basins or on steep mountainsides above and could only be reached by narrow, precipitous trails. All supplies, timber, machinery, and equipment were hauled in by pack trains, and the mines could only be worked six months a year because of the deep snows and avalanches. Mine owners built a system of trams to move buckets of ore down cables to the valley below.

Lucien Nunn achieved business success in Telluride through hard work, and he had an interest in the Gold King Mine, south of Telluride. Thinking it would be possible to use power generated by the South Fork of the San Miguel River, Nunn gathered a group of young graduate engineers who were willing to ignore old theories and try new solutions to problems. Learning as they went, the young men who called themselves "Pinheads" taught themselves about wiring, insulating and repairing, took courses in machinery and woodworking, and laid four thousand feet of pipe to conduct water to two Pelton water wheels. They climbed high poles and learned how to string electrical wires.

In 1891, Nunn built a power plant at Ames, a tiny town on the San Miguel River, and equipped it with a high-voltage, alternating current–generating motor. Nicola Tesla, the genius of alternating current, designed and built this first prototype that could generate and transmit electricity over long distances for industrial purposes. The Pinheads strung copper transmission wires over three miles from Ames up a mountain to the Gold King Mine at twelve thousand feet. On June 21, 1891, when Nunn threw the switch, a powerful jet of water hit the large Pelton wheel that was belted to the generator. A brilliant arc shot six feet into the air as everyone gasped, and within the blink

Many of Telluride's original Victorian homes and buildings are included in a National Historic District. *Courtesy of Wendy Williams.*

of an eye, the Gold King Mine had electrical power to operate its hoists and ore crushers. This was the first long-distance transmission of alternating current power in the world. The cost of operating mining machinery at the Gold King dropped immediately from $2,500 a month to $500. This electric power would be the salvation of the mining industry and transform the use of commercial electrical power forever. This was a huge stimulus to the mining industry as electric power was brought to the Tomboy, the Smuggler and the other high-altitude Telluride mines. Transmission lines were run from the plant at Ames to Telluride, and the Telluride Electric Light and Power Company was organized. Telluride became the first town in the world to become electrified with alternating current generated by falling water. It could even boast of having electric lights before New York or Paris.

In the fall of 1891, the Rio Grande Southern Railroad arrived in Telluride, beginning an economic boom. Now ore from the San Miguel Mining District could be transported quickly to Durango's smelters by rail, greatly improving the mines' profitability. Droves of immigrants from Scandinavia, France, Germany, Italy, Cornwall, and China came, seeking their fortunes. Telluride soon had over ninety businesses, including blacksmiths, hardware stores, grocery and drugstores, livery stables, barbershops, a furniture store, a brewery, and several laundries, one church, one school, and numerous saloons.

Telluride's sporting district on Pacific Street, known as "Popcorn Alley," was lined on both sides with "cribs," the small one- or two-room houses where prostitutes conducted business. There were about one hundred women here in 1899. The wealthy madams ruled the fancy parlor houses with their orchestras, wine rooms, and plush parlors. Each madam paid $150 a week to operate, and these fees helped keep the town running. The madam, in turn, charged each girl weekly "rent." The girls who didn't make the grade in the posh parlor houses worked in the Silver Belle Saloon and Dance Hall or the Senate Saloon, both of which had brothels upstairs. Known as "female boarding houses," they were still a step above the Popcorn Alley cribs.

The repeal of the Sherman Silver Purchase Act in 1893 dealt a crippling blow to silver mining in Colorado. Men were put out of work as silver mines closed, while those producing lead, copper, and zinc continued to operate. By the beginning of the twentieth century, there were serious labor disputes in the mines. Underground workers labored ten to twelve hours for less than three dollars a shift and had to pay mine owners one dollar a day for their room and board. Due to the mines' remote locations, most workers had to stay in the boardinghouses while they were working. Conditions were treacherous in the mines, and when the Smuggler-Union introduced a system greatly reducing pay, the men in the Western Federation of Miners went on strike in 1901. The violence escalated, and in 1903, the Colorado National Guard was called out by Governor Peabody, who was strongly anti-union.

Martial law was declared in Telluride, and a military pass was required to be on the street. Union members were beaten, thrown on trains and deported to towns at least fifty miles away. In a futile attempt to keep them from returning, "Fort Peabody" was built on top of thirteen-thousand-foot-high Imogene Pass, blocking a trail into Telluride. The town remained in a state of siege for fifteen months until December 1904 when the $3.00 wage was reinstated. The men went back to work facing the same dangerous conditions in the mines. Despite the labor trouble, Telluride's mines produced more than $16 million in gold and silver between 1905 and 1911.

Nature created plenty of trouble in the San Juan Mountains, which receive the most snowfall in the Rockies and are one of the earth's most dangerous avalanche regions. The avalanches were a constant threat to miners and pack trains and created havoc with the railroads, often completely blocking or tearing up the tracks. Early on the morning of February 28, 1902, the night shift of the Liberty Bell Mine had just crawled into their beds in the boardinghouse, while the day shift miners filed into the dining hall for breakfast, when a massive avalanche hit without warning. It started high above on the mountainside, uprooting trees, splintering their massive trunks, tossing huge boulders in the air and creating a seventy-five-foot-wide wall of snow. With a terrible roar, it swept three huge mine buildings into the valley below, tossing debris and bodies about. The alarm was sounded in Telluride, and soon a rescue crew, armed with picks, shovels, and dynamite, was on the way, winding up the trail to the Liberty Bell. A dozen miners had been dug out of the snow when a second avalanche roared down the slopes, burying twenty-four rescuers. The survivors searched frantically, pulling all but two out of the suffocating snow. As the weary men were dragging injured miners and the dead back down the mountain on sleds, a third avalanche swept down, burying several more. Historian David Lavender described one man "saving himself by grabbing a tree as he was being hurled down a hillside; there he clung, deafened and semiconscious, almost suffocated by the snow that had packed like cement into his ears, mouth, and nose." The deadly Liberty Bell avalanches continued for days, making rescue work impossible, and several bodies weren't recovered until summer. Twenty-four men were killed, and many more were injured in this avalanche disaster.

Three days after the Liberty Bell tragedy, there were several more avalanches that killed workers at nearby Pandora and swept away buildings at the Smuggler-Union Mine. The storm continued to pound the San Juans as the "White Death" crashed down mountainsides, sweeping away miners, rescue parties and people trying to reach the safety of towns. The railroads ground to a stop, isolating Silverton and Telluride.

The first decade of the twentieth century ended disastrously when the dam on a nearby lake burst, sending torrents of water crashing down the San Miguel River. It damaged the Ames power plant and tore up miles of railroad track, isolating Telluride. Then in July 1914, there were tremendous cloudbursts with torrential rain that overflowed creeks and rivers, sending water sweeping down Cornet Creek, smashing through a dam. A rushing wall of water, filled with tumbling boulders and ripped-up trees roared down Colorado Avenue, sweeping homes and businesses away. The lower floors of the Miners' Union Hospital and the New Sheridan Hotel were filled with twelve feet of thick mud, and Colorado Avenue was blocked by a five-foot-high wall of tangled debris. Luckily, only one person was killed in the disaster.

Many homes were swept away in the devastating Cornet Creek Flood of July 27, 1914. *Courtesy of Denver Public Library–Western History Collection.*

When Colorado enacted Prohibition in 1916, many saloons closed, while others operated as soda parlors. Telluride's city treasury quickly levied special license fees on soda parlors to replace the lost liquor establishment fees. Since law enforcement was very lax, the town's stone brewery continued churning out suds, and stills popped up in the hidden gulches. Moonshiners produced so much hooch that they were able to ship their choice batches to New York City. Al Capone bought large quantities of booze, and private clubs in Denver proudly served "Telluride Shine."

Bootlegging helped the town survive during the late 1920s when the mines started shutting down because of the low prices of gold and silver. It was a dark day in the struggling town when the stock market collapsed in 1929, and as businesses failed, the population plummeted to six hundred. As banks closed their doors, depositors lost all their money. The president of the Bank of Telluride, Charles "Buck" Waggoner, concocted an elaborate scheme using secret bank codes to swindle six of the largest financial institutions in New York City of $500,000. He used the money to cover losses in the Bank of Telluride and to repay his depositors, saving the hard-earned wages of the miners and the town's citizens. When the scheme was finally discovered, the press gleefully reported the story about a little country banker who'd fooled the wealthy New York bankers. He was compared to Robin Hood, who stole from the rich and gave money to the poor. Everyone in Telluride was very grateful to Waggoner for salvaging their funds, but the big banks were furious, and he spent several years in prison.

During the 1930s and 1940s, the old mine and mill tailings were reworked, yielding valuable base metals and gold, but this wasn't enough to keep the town going. The Idarado Mining Company purchased the Telluride mines and connected them to large mines at Red Mountain with a five-mile-long tunnel through the mountain. The Idarado mines and mill operated until 1978 but then shut down operations, and the population fell to around four hundred. Many feared it was only a matter of time before Telluride became a ghost town.

Telluride was resurrected in the 1970s by another kind of gold: "white gold," better known as snow. The new ski resort reshaped the economy, revived the Telluride community, and put the town back on the map. In 1978, two Colorado natives, Ron Allred and Jim Wells, with the backing of their Benchmark Corporation, assumed control of the ski area. They built Mountain Village, a resort with a first-class ski area, installed snowmaking equipment and lifts, and carved out new beginner terrain. In 1996, a gondola was installed to connect this luxury community with the town of Telluride, now a National Historic District.

New Sheridan Hotel

The two-story wood frame Sheridan Hotel was built in 1891, but it was destroyed by fire in 1894. It was rebuilt with bricks in 1895 and became the "New Sheridan." The front entrance opened into the elegant saloon with its calfskin wall coverings and mahogany and cherrywood bar imported from Austria. The matching back bar had large Corinthian columns framing the thirty-foot-long diamond dust mirror from France. Brass chandeliers cast a warm light on the pressed-metal ceiling, and the popular bar was separated from the lobby by leaded glass room dividers. Sparkling ore specimens from local mines were displayed in glass cases in the impressively furnished lobby. A third floor was added in 1899, and the hotel had electricity and modern plumbing with steam heat.

The New Sheridan was known all over Colorado for its delicious cuisine— said to surpass Denver's Brown Palace. Oysters, fancy ices, caviar, and lobster were packed in ice and shipped by rail to Telluride for lavish banquets and grand balls. Waiters in tuxedos served guests truffles and quail on fine china, while the snooty sommelier extoled the virtues of selections from one of the West's finest wine cellars. The Japanese pastry chef whipped up extravagant desserts for diners, some of whom had been grateful for biscuits and beans before a lucky strike made them millionaires.

Wealthy business men took their wives to dinner in the mirror-lined American Room and then danced the night away to tunes played by musicians seated in the balcony. They met their mistresses in the more intimate Continental Room, which had a discrete rear entrance. There were sixteen private dining booths, draped in heavy, plush velvet, ideal for cozy tête-à-têtes. Every booth had its own telephone that could be used to summon a waiter when he was needed—and to avoid any embarrassing interruptions.

In October 1903, three-time presidential candidate William Jennings Bryan spoke to a huge crowd of supporters from a grandstand in front of the New Sheridan. He delivered a reprise of his stirring "Cross of Gold Speech"

In 1903, William Jennings Bryan addressed a crowd in front of the New Sheridan Hotel. *Courtesy of History Colorado.*

The New Sheridan Hotel on Colorado Avenue is popular with locals and tourists. *Courtesy of Wendy Williams.*

supporting free silver, which he'd originally given at the 1896 Democratic convention in Chicago.

The hotel hosted Lillian Russell, Sarah Bernhardt, Lillian Gish, newspaperman Damon Runyon, and Eugene Debbs, the union leader. During the Telluride labor struggles in 1903–4, when the town was under martial law, federal troops took over the hotel for their headquarters. They even imprisoned a union leader, Charles Moyer, for six months in an upstairs hotel room.

The New Sheridan fell on hard times in the 1940s when many large mines stopped producing lead and other metals, sending Telluride into a decline. The hotel changed hands several times, but it was neglected and most of its fine furniture was sold to Knott's Berry Farm in California. In 1977, a new owner completely renovated the hotel and furnished it with fine antiques. The elaborate Victorian wallpaper was replaced with an elegant replica, and today the historic saloon looks just as it did in 1895. There's fine dining in the Chop House and the Parlor, or guests can eat while they soak up the sunshine and mountain views on The Roof. The hotel is part of the National Historic District and is listed on the National Trust for Historic Hotels of America

Ghosts

The New Sheridan, like many hotels that date back a century or more, has a few guests who've remained through the years. There are unexplained creaks and groans, quiet footsteps in the night, cold drafts, and mysterious shadows. The hotel was investigated in 2011 by StanJan Paranormal, who posted their findings on YouTube. Antonio Garcez, author of *Colorado Ghost Stories*, interviewed a maid at the hotel who told him about her strange experience. She had closed and locked the door of a vacant room when she suddenly saw a man walk right through the door. He didn't speak, walked by, and went to the end of the hall where he passed right through the exterior wall. Frightened, she screamed for her co-worker, who told her about some of her own strange experiences. This other housekeeper had been cleaning a room when she heard a man speaking to her. No one was around, and the room was empty. Frightened, she hurried to finish when a man started singing an old song, "Rosemarie, why don't you dance with me?" She stopped her work again to make sure the hall and the nearby rooms were empty. She found no one. She was serenaded several different mornings, and there was never anyone around. Sometimes she heard a light cough and sounds like someone was clearing his throat repeatedly.

12
DOLORES

Dolores is a tiny town nestled in a canyon of the San Juan Mountains with the Dolores River running along one side and rocky cliffs on the other. The people who live here are proud of their town, its four parks, the library, and the Galloping Goose Historical Society Museum. The Galloping Goose is a resourceful combination of a Buick or Pierce-Arrow body and an enclosed truck bed that was used to carry, mail, freight, and passengers on the tracks of the Rio Grande Southern Railroad. The first Goose was built in 1931 and delivered mail to the mountain towns. There were seven Geese operating in Southern Colorado until the 1950s, when the railroad lost the mail contract. The Geese were converted for tourist use and carried passengers on the Durango-Silverton Narrow Gauge Railroad and the Cumbres-Toltec Railroad.

Centuries before the railroad came to southwestern Colorado, the Ancient Puebloans built their adobe homes high in the cliffs above the canyons of Mesa Verde. Their civilization flourished for hundreds of years but mysteriously vanished by AD 1300. The Spanish explorers came in the 1500s, looking for cities of gold, but when they found only adobe pueblos, they didn't return for two centuries. In 1765, Don Juan de Maria de Rivera led an exploring party into the San Juan Mountains, looking for gold and silver. They left some evidence of their early mining efforts and named several of the area's rivers: the San Juan, the Rio de las Animas (the River of Lost Souls), the Mancos (the River of the Crippled One), and the Rio de Nuestra Senora de las Dolores (the River of Sorrow).

HAUNTED HOTELS OF SOUTHERN COLORADO

Galloping Goose #5 carried mail, passengers, and freight for the Rio Grande Southern Railroad. *Courtesy of Wendy Williams.*

In the 1870s, the water of the Dolores River and the lush grass lining its banks drew cattlemen to the Dolores Valley. The little town of Big Bend was settled in a sweeping curve of the Dolores River, and it grew very slowly due to its isolation. There was a constant threat of attack by the Utes, whose hunting parties roamed the valley and frightened the settlers working in their fields. Afraid that the Indians would torch their cabins while they were sleeping, the settlers often hid outside in the brush at night. Investors refused to go where "savages lurked," and the ranchers didn't want any Utes for neighbors, certain they were stealing their horses and slaughtering their cattle.

By 1881, most of the Utes had been pushed out of Colorado and sent to a reservation in Utah, only the Southern Utes remained on a reservation southwest of Durango. Treaties had established their right to leave the reservation to hunt, but this increased tensions with the farmers and ranchers. On June 19, 1885, a group of white cattlemen attacked an Indian hunting party at their camp on Beaver Creek, north of Dolores. They killed six Utes and wounded two others, then they fled. A few days later, in retaliation, a party of Utes attacked a settler's homestead, burning his cabin, killing the father and seriously wounding the mother, who managed to escape with her children. Once again, settlers fled their homes to hide in the brush as troopers from Fort Lewis, near Durango, patrolled the Dolores area. Suspicious ranchers quickly threw together a log fort where the settlers took refuge.

Newspapers as far off as Denver raged and demanded that the Indian atrocities must be stopped, completely ignoring the fact that the Indians had been attacked first and were the victims at Beaver Creek. The June 23, 1885 *Durango Ideal* insisted, "The progressive white people and the lousey [*sic*] greasy Indians cannot occupy this country together." Editorials shouted for the complete removal of the Utes from their Southern Colorado reservation. They cited the fate of the Northern Utes, who'd been removed from Colorado and placed on the Uintah reservation in Utah.

As the months went by, calm gradually returned to the Dolores Valley. The whites who had killed the Indians at Beaver Creek were never identified, and the Utes' off-reservation activities were restricted. The relations between the

The Rio Grande Southern Railroad Depot at Dolores displays nineteenth-century railroad memorabilia. *Courtesy of Wendy Williams.*

two factions did not improve, but as the years passed, the hostility slowly lessened, and the shame of the Beaver Creek Massacre gradually faded.

The small town of Big Bend had three general merchandise stores, a blacksmith, a livery stable, and one saloon by 1884. Cattle ranching was the leading business in the Dolores River Valley, and the first herds of Shorthorns and Herefords were introduced. They could survive the severe winters and high altitude better than other breeds, and the herds multiplied. The mining camps in the nearby San Juans were lucrative markets for meat, hay, and farm produce, but the cattlemen also needed a means of transportation to the eastern markets.

When the railroad arrived in Durango in 1881, cattle from Dolores ranches were driven to its depot, loaded on the train and shipped to Denver and St. Louis. In 1891, the Rio Grande Southern Railroad established its railhead a few miles east of Big Bend and built a depot there. Most of Big Bend's merchants packed up their goods and moved to the tiny new town, which they named "Dolores." The majority of Big Bend's citizens followed, and Dolores grew slowly. It survived the closure of the silver mines, the Great Depression, and two world wars. Today, it is the center of a recreational paradise of fishing and hunting, hiking, climbing, and outdoor activities.

Rio Grande Southern Hotel

Opportunity arrived in Dolores with the Rio Grande Southern Railroad, and early settler E.L. Wilbur seized it. He quickly remodeled his own family home, built in 1873, into Dolores's first hotel. Wilbur opened the Rio Grande Southern Hotel in 1893, and it was a great success. The guest rooms were clean, and Mrs. Wilbur served delicious, home-cooked meals. Two trains arrived daily from Durango. The first came at noon, and the passengers were eager to stretch their legs and have lunch at the hotel. The second train from Durango pulled in around 8:00 p.m., and its passengers spent the night at the hotel. Railroad conductors, engineers, and others who worked for the Rio Grande Southern happily joined their passengers for a night at the hotel. Then everyone continued on their journey or their job the next morning. Railroad workers who were laying tracks from Dolores north to Telluride boarded at the hotel until the line was completed.

Dolores had no newspaper, so the hotel lobby became a popular place where townspeople mingled with travelers and caught up on the news. The

The Rio Grande Southern Hotel was a welcome stop for passengers traveling on the Rio Grande Southern. Railroad. *Courtesy of Wendy Williams.*

hotel, whose name was often abbreviated to "The Southern," was the only one in town and, as a major employer, very important to the local economy. Today, the hotel is one of Dolores's oldest businesses, located in one of the original buildings.

In 1906, Teddy Roosevelt made the hotel his headquarters when he visited Mesa Verde before designating it as a national park. Western novelist Zane Grey came to research the area in 1911 and wrote several chapters of his bestselling novel, *Riders of the Purple Sage*, while sitting at a desk in room no. 4. During the 1920s, when the region's shale oil business was booming, Conoco and Texaco employees often boarded here.

The Rio Grande Southern has had several owners over the years, and at one time, its restaurant offered a popular Friday night fish fry. Locals flocked to the hotel to enjoy the food and the hand-crafted beer created by a local brew master. Chef-writer Rita Bergstrom operated the Old German Restaurant at the hotel for nearly a decade and wrote her bestselling cookbook, *Taste of Old Germany*, while working there.

Ghosts

Today, some of the hotel rooms are rented by permanent residents, while others are reserved for travelers and tourists. Everyone living at the hotel has heard the strange stories about its ghosts, and some have even encountered these apparitions. The hotel has been investigated by a paranormal group that determined several different spirits reside here. Some people have seen the apparition of a young teenage girl on the second floor as she dashes about and then vanishes. Occasionally, she appears in a guest room but disappears quickly.

When the hotel was being renovated, a tall stranger, who was often seen carrying a ladder, came and went. Construction workers and the hotel owner thought he was one of the workmen hired for the project. Then one day he walked right through a wall in front of several stunned employees. Guests and residents have seen a wispy, elderly gentleman who resembles an old photo of a local physician. Many years ago, the doctor married the woman who owned the Southern Hotel at the time. The couple lived there for several years.

13
DELTA

Delta sits in an area of rich soil and fine silt deposits where the Gunnison and Uncompahgre Rivers come together. Antoine Robidoux, a trader from Santa Fe, built Fort Uncompahgre, near the south bank of the Gunnison River in 1828. There was plenty of wood for building, campfires, and heating and lots of grass for the horses of the Utes who came to the fort, eager to trade, especially for guns. Robidoux established several routes that he used to haul goods from St. Louis and Santa Fe to his trading post. The Mountain Branch of the Spanish Trail was much shorter, but it was very difficult. It ran north from Santa Fe, through the San Luis Valley of Southern Colorado, across Cochetopa Pass into the Gunnison River Valley to the fort. The other route, known as Robidoux's Cutoff, was shorter, and the trader used it when he was bringing guns and goods from St. Louis. This trail bypassed Santa Fe and avoided customs with its high taxes.

The Utes traded their animal pelts and hides for guns, blankets, knives, tobacco, cloth, and beads. The sale or trade of guns was prohibited by both Spanish and Mexican law, but enforcement at remote Fort Uncompahgre was nearly impossible. Robidoux operated his trading post with about fifteen Mexican employees until 1843. That summer, trouble between the Utes and the Mexicans in Santa Fe broke out, and warfare spread through Southern Colorado to the Robidoux post. The Utes attacked the post and killed fourteen of his Mexican employees and seized all of the women. Only one worker escaped the carnage and managed to reach Taos two weeks later.

Antoine Robidoux had not been at the fort when the Indians attacked, and he never returned to the area, completely abandoning his business. The Utes later let him know their anger had been directed at the Mexicans, not him, and asked him to return. Robidoux refused, and about two years after the massacre, the Utes burned down the fort buildings.

In October 1881, when the Northern Utes were driven from Colorado and placed on the Uintah Reservation in Utah, settlers, town builders, farmers, and ranchers rushed to grab their lands. By the end of September 1882, all the choice parcels near the rivers had been taken. Delta County was created by the legislature in February 1883, with the county seat of Uncompahgre City. Since its citizens couldn't spell or pronounce that name, the town soon became "Delta" because of its location at the confluence of the two rivers.

The Uncompahgre Valley around Delta and Montrose is very dry, receiving an average of seven inches of rain per year. The soil was rich, but water for irrigation was needed before any crops could be grown. Farmers dug ditches from the Uncompahgre River to the fields and planted their crops. Their first harvests were enormous, so more land was plowed, and more fields were planted, extending from Delta to Montrose. The valley produced all types of fruits and vegetables, including potatoes, onions, cherries, apples, corn, wheat, and other grains.

By 1909, the Denver & Rio Grande Railroad had completed its tracks through the valley and was carrying produce and livestock to markets in Denver and the mountain mining towns. The valley had over 5,700 bee colonies, and its honey won first place at the 1904 Chicago World's Fair. Sugar beets thrived around Delta, and Holly Sugar built a large processing plant there in 1920.

As the number of established farms increased, it became obvious that the Uncompahgre River could not provide enough water for irrigation. The water supply dwindled, crops dried up, and families were forced to abandon their once productive farms. For twenty years, farmers in the dry valley struggled with the lack of water. They knew that just sixteen miles away there was plenty of water in the Gunnison River, which ran through the Black Canyon. A massive mountain range blocked this water from reaching the thirsty Uncompahgre Valley fields.

In 1904, a proposal for a large ditch to carry water from the Gunnison River was discarded in favor of boring a tunnel through the mountains. The United States Reclamation Service began the Gunnison Tunnel Project in 1905, and it took four years to complete. President William

Workers unloading railroad carloads of sugar beets for processing at the Holly Sugar plant at Delta. *Courtesy of History Colorado.*

Howard Taft presided at the opening ceremonies for the 5.8-mile-long tunnel. It would enough carry water to irrigate 146,000 acres of farmland in Delta, Montrose, and Ouray Counties. The completion of Blue Mesa Reservoir and Dam in 1965 augmented the Western Slope's water supply and supported growth in Delta, Paonia, Crawford, and the small agricultural towns. Now the orchards surrounding Delta produce two-thirds of Colorado's apple crop, as well as apricots, cherries, nectarines, peaches, and plums.

During the 1980s, Delta began a project to give its Main Street a facelift. With financial help from the National Trust for Historic Preservation, more than one hundred trees were planted and a dozen murals were painted on the downtown buildings. In 1992, Delta won an All-American City award. The Delta County Historical Society Museum has many artifacts from the town's early years, and it is especially proud of its collection of dinosaur bones that were found in this area.

The Historical Society is responsible for the care of the Council Tree, a cottonwood tree believed to be at least 215 years old. It is the sole survivor of an ancient grove located near a Ute trail and was an important meeting place for the Native Americans. The local chapter of the DAR recognized this historic connection to the Utes by placing a bronze plaque on the Council Tree in the 1930s. Through the years, strong winds and harsh weather have

The Ute Council Tree is over two hundred years old and was a favorite meeting place of the Indians. *Courtesy of Wendy Williams.*

taken their toll on this tree, and the last living branch broke off and fell in August 2017. In the interest of public safety, the historical society decided to cut the top portion of the ancient tree down, leaving only a twenty-eight-foot-high trunk.

FAIRLAMB BED + BREAKFAST

The Fairlamb home was built by Millard and Stella Fairlamb in 1906, using locally manufactured bricks. The three-story, American Foursquare home sits on a bluff overlooking the delta formed by the Gunnison and Uncompahgre Rivers. Brothers, sisters, and other relatives of Millard and Stella built their homes along this street until the residences of the Fairlamb clan covered an entire city block.

The Fairlambs lived in this house for many years and raised their children here. Millard died in 1947, but Stella lived until 1968. Their home was passed down to their children and then their grandchildren and remained in the Fairlamb family for seventy-two years. The house was purchased around 1978 by two local physicians, who used it as a rental home. They had a number of different tenants over the years and sold it in February 1994 to Elizabeth Thompson and John Taylor.

The years had taken their toll on the house, and it was desperately in need of repairs and a major renovation. Its rather plain American design was a contrast to the more ornate Victorian style of the 1890s and early 1900s. The

The Fairlamb House is a combination of American Four Square and Arts and Crafts architectural styles. *Courtesy of Wendy Williams.*

Pump organs were often played in family homes in the nineteenth century. *Courtesy of Wendy Williams.*

house incorporated features of the Prairie and Arts and Crafts styles, which are characterized by a square, boxy house with dormers, a hipped roof, and plenty of Craftsman woodwork. Many of the original fixtures and special features of this home were gone, so replacements were salvaged from older buildings of the same period. The entry and front hall light fixtures came from an old school building in Washington State. An Arts and Crafts–style stained-glass and brass light fixture was once in an old Denver commercial building. The handsome grandfather clock was made by Elizabeth's father, and the front door, inlaid hardwood floors, and the Arts and Crafts–style fireplace are original.

Today, the Fairlamb House is operated as a bed-and-breakfast. John and Elizabeth have maintained its post-Victorian style with antique furnishings and lace-curtained windows. There's a vintage pump organ in the inviting library, where guests can relax and browse through the books.

There are three guest rooms on the third floor with two bathrooms, one with a claw-footed bathtub. The pastel flower wallpaper and white wrought-iron bedframe in the Stella Room contrast with the dark, wooden furniture in the Millard Room. The smaller Ethel Room has a brass bed with a canopy, and interestingly, the closet in this room was once a connecting passageway to the bedroom next door. A century ago, this was referred to as a "discretion closet."

Ghosts

The Fairlamb family really did have a skeleton—not in their closet but in their attic. Millard, who built the house, had a deep interest in the ancient tribes that lived in adobe cliff dwellings for centuries. He often searched for their ruins and artifacts, and on a trip to Utah, he found a human skeleton. Instead of notifying the authorities, he gathered up the bones, put them in a box, and took them home. Millard stored this box of bones in his attic, where they scared children who were bold enough to peek. The bones remained in the attic for years until they were given to the Utes for a proper burial. Now some people speculate that a wandering spirit may have been attached to these ancient bones, and it still hangs around the house.

Just a few years after John and Elizabeth purchased the home, they had Native American guests who were attending the Council Tree Pow Wow and Festival that's held in Delta every fall. After spending one night in the Millard Room, the guests, a Lakota medicine man and his wife, said that the spirits of five women were trapped in the house. They had awakened to see these apparitions standing at their bedside. The medicine man performed a cleansing ceremony and smudged the entire house with burning sage. Then he called upon the angels and free spirits to help these trapped ghosts move on.

The apparitions of several ladies, wearing fashions of the early 1900s, have been seen around the house. They appear most often in the Millard Room but vanish quickly when they're noticed. A rocking chair quietly moves back and forth when no one's near, and the bathroom lights often flicker on and off. There's been similar activity in both the Ethel and Stella bedrooms. Strange cold spots are noticed throughout the house, while disembodied voices, banging sounds, and mysterious footsteps are heard.

A pretty little seashell is often mysteriously moved around from place to place. It might be left on a shelf in one room, only to show up in an odd

A lot of paranormal activity has been noticed in the Millard Room. *Courtesy of Wendy Williams.*

place in another room the following day. Occasionally, someone says they feel like they are being watched, or they sense an unseen presence. Some people theorize that the pieces salvaged from other vintage buildings may have come to the Fairlamb House with an attached spirit. When a team investigated the paranormal activity, they heard about a death years ago when a family member suffered a fatal fall from a ladder while hanging Christmas ornaments. They wonder if this tragedy might be responsible for the unexplained paranormal activity? Could the restless spirits in this house be related to the old bones that were stored in the attic?

A team of paranormal investigators recorded wide variations on their EMF (electromagnetic field) meters in the bedrooms. They recorded several different voices that were picked up by their spirit box in these rooms. They were able to identify the words, "girl, ghosts, blood, death," and "bones," all given in response to their questions.

14

GRAND JUNCTION

Generations of Utes lived in the lands along the western slope of the Rockies, spending the winters in the sheltered lower valleys and moving their tipis to the high mesas when the snows melted. Then in the mid-sixteenth century, Spanish explorers came north into the Rio Grande Valley, looking for elusive cities of gold and bringing the first horses. These horses changed the Utes' way of life, and they became excellent horsemen, ranging far afield in search of game and their enemies. They unified into bands and became more aggressive against others who trespassed on their territory.

For many years, few white men ventured across the Continental Divide into the northern portion of the Colorado Territory after the Pike's Peak Gold Rush of 1859. This was the land of the Ute tribes, and they did not welcome intruders. The 1870s discovery of gold and silver in the San Juan Mountains eventually led to a series of treaties with these Indians which affected all of the land west of the Continental Divide. The Utes gave up large chunks of territory and were pushed onto reservations. Tensions between the white settlers and the Indians increased, exploding in the Meeker Massacre of 1879. The result of this tragedy was the forcible removal of most Utes from Colorado by 1881.

Once the Utes were gone, farmers and ranchers rushed to claim the fertile land at the juncture of the Grand (Colorado) and Gunnison Rivers. George Crawford, William McGinley, J. Clayton Nichols, and four other settlers bought a large amount of land, formed the Grand Junction Land Company

City lots were sold at the Grand Junction Land office in 1882. *Courtesy of Denver Public Library–Western History Collection.*

and laid out a town site in September 1882. Crawford helped design the city's irrigation system and started work on the Grand River Ditch, which was completed in 1884. It was thirty-five feet wide and carried water twenty-four miles from Palisade to irrigate the orchards. This made large-scale farming possible. The Denver & Rio Grande Railroad arrived in November 1882, and the following year, the legislature created Mesa County. It was named for the world's largest flat-topped mountain, Grand Mesa.

The first Grand Junction settlers lived in tents until they could build log houses. There was plenty of wood in the groves of large cottonwood trees growing along the river. A lumber mill opened in 1882, and then Kimball's brickyard began turning out materials for the first permanent buildings. Entire blocks had been set aside for schools and municipal buildings, and by 1882, the new city hall had been completed. Churches were built, a newspaper was founded, and soon there were solid brick business buildings and a bank lining Colorado Avenue.

Grand Junction became a hub for the railroad and a regional supply center after the D&RG arrived, loaded with agricultural supplies and equipment. Fruit, agricultural produce, and livestock were shipped to Denver and eastern markets from Grand Junction. The town became an oasis in the desert as more irrigation ditches were dug. They carried water to lawns, gardens, and the numerous trees that had been planted to shade the city's streets and parks.

The Grand Valley is protected by several high plateaus that make it ideal for agriculture. There are the Book Cliffs to the north, Grand Mesa to the east, and the Uncompahgre Plateau to the southwest. The towering sandstone monoliths and deep canyons that became Colorado National Monument in 1911 are west of the valley. These high plateaus surrounding the Grand Valley are covered with snow until late spring, keeping the cool air in the valley below. This prevents the trees from blooming too soon and then freezing in one of Colorado's late spring snow storms. Frosts are very rare, making this an ideal place to raise peaches, pears, apricots, and cherries.

Grapes were planted on the Western Slope in 1899, and they thrived. The vineyards developed into a booming business until Prohibition arrived, and the vines were ripped from the ground by government agents. Even though Prohibition was repealed in 1933, it took over seventy years for the wine industry to become reestablished here. Today, grapes are being grown in the world's highest-altitude vineyards near Paonia and Hotchkiss. The vineyards around Palisade and Grand Junction produce 85 to 95 percent of Colorado's grapes.

Sugar beets did well in Grand Junction's mild climate, and the first processing plant, Colorado Sugar Manufacturing Company, opened in 1899. It was sold in 1916 to Holly Sugar, which operated it until 1929, when the company consolidated its operations at Delta. The plant building sat vacant in Grand Junction until the uranium boom of the 1950s, when it was used as a mill to process carnotite ore for vanadium and uranium.

The atomic bomb blasted the world into a new era, the Cold War, in 1947. It also started a new boom in Colorado that had all the craziness of the gold and silver rushes of the previous century. The magic word was *uranium* during the 1950s. Hopeful uranium prospectors could buy a government "how-to" pamphlet, purchase a Geiger counter, and head off to the Colorado Plateau or Four Corners and make a lucky strike.

The Atomic Energy Commission and several uranium mining companies directed field activities from their offices in Grand Junction, and the town became the epicenter of activity for weekend prospectors. The excitement reached a fever pitch in uranium-crazed towns, as investors threw their money around wildly, buying stocks in mining companies and processing mills. As the boom continued, more geologists, mining engineers, and wealthy businessmen came to town, increasing its economic growth.

As uranium stockpiles grew, the government's need decreased. In 1962, the uranium rush slowed when the Vanadium Corporation closed down its operations and left. Many Western Slope towns that had rushed to open

The Western Slope produced record crops of sugar beets. *Courtesy of Denver Public Library–Western History Collection.*

uranium-processing mills were left with radioactive mine dumps and tailings. Miners were facing health problems from working in the uranium mines.

This boom-and-bust cycle continued during the 1970s when oil was discovered in northwestern Colorado, and the Green River Basin oil-shale deposits were found. The development of these resources boosted the economy until extraction costs exceeded the falling price of oil. Then ExxonMobile left the area, jobs were lost, and again there was a great deal of economic hardship around Grand Junction.

Today, Grand Junction is the most populous city on the Western Slope, and it has become a major commercial and transportation center. Thousands of outdoor recreation enthusiasts raft the Colorado River, hike on Grand Mesa, and explore Colorado National Monument. This area is very popular with mountain bikers, and the Kokopelli Trail runs about 150 miles from town across the desert to Moab, Utah. This is the state's major fruit-growing region, and it is the center of Colorado's wine industry.

MELROSE HOTEL

The Melrose Hotel was built in 1909 on Colorado Avenue, the main street, by James Ponsford and his two sons. Ponsford knew the hotel business well since he'd worked as a porter in several London establishments. In 1884, he brought his wife and three-month-old daughter to America, and they immediately headed west to Colorado. Ponsford thought Grand Junction offered the promise of a profitable future and the possibility of owning a hotel.

James filed a land claim on Kannah Creek, where there was plenty of water and rich soil. The young couple had four more children and farmed for twenty-four years, saving their money until they could buy a lot on Colorado Avenue in 1904. William and his two eldest sons, George and James, dug their hotel basement by hand and started purchasing bricks. It took them four more years to build the hotel, brick by brick. In 1908, the two-story brick building was finally completed with ten rooms, including the family's living quarters. In 1911, they bought the adjacent lot and built an addition, doubling their hotel's size to twenty-eight rooms.

The hotel's home-like atmosphere attracted travelers, and as Grand Junction grew, railroad men, agricultural produce buyers, cattlemen, and sugar beet investors stayed there. The hotel was downtown near the railroad depot and the bank, and the Ponsfords' business became profitable.

The family made many building improvements, and by the late 1920s, every guest room had a sink with running water, a rarity in Grand Junction at that time. The hotel remained in the Ponsford family for many years, passing down from father to sons. When it was almost one hundred years old in 1994, great-granddaughter Mary Davi sold the hotel to a married couple, Sabrina and Marcus Bebb-Jones.

The couple operated the business for about three years until there was a tragedy. Sabrina disappeared while on a family outing in the desert, and although authorities spent days searching, she wasn't found. Suspicion fell on Sabrina's husband, Marcus, whose explanations didn't seem believable. Then in September 1997, Marcus spent several days gambling and partying in Las Vegas. He rented a room in a luxury hotel, wrote a farewell note to his three-year-old son, Daniel, and then shot himself. His wound was superficial, and lawmen decided this was just an attempt to divert attention from the search for his wife.

Despite all the hours spent combing the rugged desert, Sabrina's body was not found, and no criminal evidence was ever turned up. Marcus Bebb-

The downtown location of the Melrose Hotel was convenient for businessmen and merchants. *Courtesy of Wendy Williams.*

Jones returned to his native England with his young son and moved in with his grandmother. He left the responsibility of raising his son to her and embarked on a career as a professional poker player.

In 2004, a cattle rancher found a skull in a remote meadow in nearby Garfield County. Forensic examination identified the skull as Sabrina's, and it had an obvious bullet hole. The police launched an investigation, chasing down clues, and finally collected enough evidence to file murder charges against Marcus Bebb-Jones. He was extradited to the United States and returned to Colorado in 2011. He pleaded guilty to second-degree murder and was sentenced to the maximum twenty years in prison.

The Melrose Hotel deteriorated for several years, and it was sold in 1998. Its new owner received a grant from the city to update the hotel's exterior. For a while, it was operated as a hostel, and the management helped people who were new to the area find jobs and permanent homes. Now this hotel is still home to some long-term residents, and it welcomes short-stay guests, who appreciate its downtown location. Most of the rooms are decorated with vintage furnishings from the early 1900s to the 1940s. Two rooms have private baths, while the remainder share the bathrooms and shower. There are sinks in most guest rooms.

Ghosts

After William Ponsford died in 1914, many friends believed that he was still around helping Charlotte and her sons operate the hotel. Charlotte died in 1932, and the hotel was inherited by the three Ponsford sons, who operated it for many years. Guests have noticed strange, shadowy figures around the hotel, and many swore they've seen a man dressed in clothes from the early 1900s. He was often seen standing at the top of the stairs, looking down into the parlor. Another man, who was thin and taller, wearing a hat, was frequently seen looking out a front window. Both apparitions faded away if they were approached but later silently reappeared.

Hotel managers became familiar with these spirits, but in the 1990s, they noticed the sounds of a woman crying. This began after Sabrina disappeared. The sobs and cries were loud in the basement, and unnerved employees notified the police. Investigators found a small pile of Sabrina's belongings wrapped up and hidden in the east corner of the basement. Employees recalled how the couple often argued about finances and

The Melrose is Grand Junction's oldest hotel and has been in continuous operation since 1908. *Courtesy of Wendy Williams.*

management of the hotel. Neither had seemed very happy. After Marcus was sentenced to prison, the crying stopped. The manager was convinced that Sabrina had been murdered in the basement, always saying, "Marcus killed her down there!"

15
PAONIA

After most of the Utes had been placed on reservations, white settlers quickly moved onto their Western Slope lands. They laid out new towns and began building homes of cottonwood logs with floors of packed dirt. The cracks between the logs were filled with adobe mud, and the walls were covered with old newspapers. The tallow candles and coal oil lamps that were used for light could be easily upset and caused many fires.

Enos Hotchkiss had made several trips over the mountains from Lake City to explore the Valley of the North Fork of the Gunnison River, but he'd been chased out by the Utes. Now in the fall of 1881, the Indians were gone, and Hotchkiss claimed land for his homestead near the site of the future town that would bear his name. Samuel Wade and William Clark, who accompanied Hotchkiss, explored farther up the North Fork Valley, claimed land and founded Paonia. They platted the new townsite, laying out the streets, business and residential lots, and even set aside land for a park.

Wade had brought root stock of his favorite flower, the peony, from Ohio. He planted the flowers on his claim and in the new park. Today, more than one hundred years later, bright peonies that are the descendants of that original root stock bloom in Paonia's Town Park. Wade wanted to name the budding town for the peony and submitted the scientific name Paeonia in the request for a post office. However, the government official misspelled the name, and the town officially became "Paonia."

In 1882, Sam Wade ordered hundreds of fruit trees from an eastern nursery, and the young trees were shipped on the railroad to the depot at

Gunnison. Wade met the train and loaded the trees carefully into his wagon, covered them with blankets, and set out for Paonia across Black Mesa. Even though it was late spring, the snow was still very deep, and Wade had to shovel a wide path through drifts before his team and wagon could make its way through. At night, he kept the trees warm by building large bonfires around the wagon. It took him three weeks to reach the North Fork Valley with the fruit trees, which were the beginnings of the orchards that thrive today around Paonia, Crawford, and Hotchkiss.

As the Denver and Rio Grande Railroad laid its tracks west from Gunnison, new towns sprang up along the rail line. A depot was built at Delta so farmers could ship their fruit, vegetables, cattle, and sheep to Denver and the eastern markets. At the 1893 Chicago Columbian Exposition, the fruit from Sam Wade's and W.S. Coburn's orchards won the first gold medals. This was quite an accomplishment for growers in an isolated Western Slope community.

Everyone packed fruit from Paonia's orchards to be shipped east on the railroad. *Courtesy of Denver Public Library–Western History Collection.*

By 1902, the narrow-gauge tracks of the Denver & Rio Grande running into the North Fork Valley were completed, and numerous carloads of fruit and vegetables were being shipped by rail. The valley became well known for its bountiful crops of apples, cherries, peaches, apricots, nectarines, grapes, and plums.

Sam Wade dug the first irrigation ditch to carry water to his orchards. By 1900, there were at least eighteen ditches under construction from the North Fork of the Gunnison River to the orchards. The completion of the Uncompahgre Project in the early 1900s provided a dependable source of water for Montrose and Delta and encouraged agriculture and growth.

Blasting the Gunnison Tunnel through miles of dense rock to bring water from the Gunnison River in the Black Canyon took four years to complete. The project included the construction of the Taylor Park Dam and Reservoir, seven diversion dams, 128 miles of main canals, 438 miles of laterals, and 216 miles of drains. The Paonia Water Project was finished in 1939 to augment the valley's water supply.

A rich seam of anthracite coal was found in the upper valley in 1883, and the town of Somerset developed around the new coal mines. By 1903, the D&RG had reached Somerset, bringing in all supplies and hauling out carloads of coal for the Denver market.

The North Valley fruit industry boomed until 1910, when prices dropped and there were spring freezes for the first time in many years. Then the cherry orchards were attacked by deadly insects, forcing farmers to pull up their trees, plow up their orchards, and use their land for farming and pasture. The years passed, and as the North Fork Valley slowly recovered from the infestation, young cherry trees were planted once again.

Today, Paonia is a quiet agricultural community at the foot of the west Elk Mountains, where the large crops of cherries are celebrated with the annual Cherry Days festivities in July. Fall brings the Mountain Harvest Festival and the hilarious Grape Stomp. Anglers have good luck fishing in the waters of the North Fork of the Gunnison River and in the Paonia Reservoir at Paonia State Park. The town is the headquarters of the *High Country News*, a publication whose serious journalists produce hard-hitting articles about environmental and economic issues affecting the West. A bit off the beaten path, Paonia has attracted artists and writers who savor its quiet country lifestyle.

Bross Hotel

In 1905, deputy sheriff William Taylor Bross, known as "WT," was always quick to seize an opportunity. Paonia needed a hotel, so WT saved his money and bought several lots on Onarga Avenue and built a three-story fireproof brick hotel. It had electricity, hot and cold running water in all the rooms, indoor plumbing, and a coal-fired furnace that kept it cozy and warm in the winter. The large bay windows allowed bright sunshine in, and guests could relax on the front porch or the second-floor veranda. The new Bross Hotel was Paonia's only "first class hotel," and it was often called "The Brown Palace of Delta County."

While WT was building the hotel, his wife, Laura, ran a boardinghouse next door and raised their six children. She was a good cook, and there were rarely any empty seats at her dinner table. The hotel opened in May 1906, and every evening, WT met the train and loaded his guests and their luggage into his wagon for the ride to the hotel. They received a warm welcome from Laura, who was known by everyone as "Mother Bross."

Left: The Bross Hotel was advertised as Paonia's only "First Class Hotel." *Courtesy of Wendy Williams.*

Right: The front porch has always been a favorite place where guests relax. *Courtesy of Wendy Williams.*

The hotel flourished for years, and after WT died in 1921, the youngest son, Otto, helped Mother Bross run the hotel. She died in 1928, and Otto remodeled the hotel and operated it successfully through the 1930s. He converted the basement into a meeting room for the Rotary Club and community events. He was friends with another bachelor, Merrill Henry, who lived at the hotel for many years until his death. In 1944, Otto sold the hotel to a buyer, who agreed that he could live there for the rest of his life. Otto never married and made his home in room 2 until he died there in 1959.

The hotel was renovated in 1997, and in 2001, it was purchased by Linda Lentz. She was very interested in the spirits that shared the hotel and wrote about her experiences in a booklet, *Bross Hotel: One Hundred Years 1906–2006*, which she gave to her guests. In 2013, the Delta County Board of County Commissioners placed the hotel on the county's Historic Landmark Register, and in 2015, the Bross Hotel was named to the National Register of Historic Places. In 2017, the hotel was sold to Kevin and Karen Kropp, who've operated an organic fruit farm in the North Fork Valley since the 1980s.

Ghosts

The Bross family lived in their boardinghouse next door to the hotel for years, and after the death of his mother, Otto sold the house. When he took over the management of the hotel and began remodeling, he decided not to make any changes in room 2. He said that he sensed a very strong presence there that wanted the room left in its original state. Through the years, this room and its number remained unchanged; the only concession to progress was the addition of a small bathroom. Many believe Mother Bross lingers in the home she loved, and she especially favors room 2, which was Otto's room. Linda Lentz often said, "She is happy in room 2….She probably haunts that room because she's looking out for her baby, Otto." Guests staying in this cozy room have felt their blankets being tucked gently around their shoulders. Most people believe that Mother Bross lingers on in this home that she loved.

A guest, who was studying an old photograph of Mother Bross and WT, made an uncomplimentary observation about Mother's looks—it was immediately punctuated by a loud crash. The antique mirror that hangs over the marble-topped buffet had suddenly fallen to the floor, despite being

An image of a woman resembling Mother Bross has been seen in this antique mirror. *Courtesy of Wendy Williams.*

bolted to the wall. Amazingly, the mirror was not cracked or broken. Fearing the spirit of Mother Bross had been offended by the remark, the innkeeper, who was a believer, rushed upstairs to room 2 where she made a sincere apology for her guest's comment. The mirror was returned to its place on the wall and has never fallen again.

Occasionally, Mother Bross likes to relax in one of the smaller rooms upstairs, and guests sometimes say they sense a presence in their room. There are indentations on beds as if someone had sat down for a minute to rest. The hotel renovations during the 1990s apparently disturbed Mother Bross and Otto because apparitions of both mother and son were seen by many different people. The basement and upper floors of the hotel experienced the greatest paranormal activity during the construction commotion.

In 1993, a single family rented the entire hotel for a short time, but the woman became very uncomfortable working in the second-floor laundry room. She insisted that someone was watching her there. She saw an apparition of a woman who resembled old photographs of Mother Bross. She was wearing a long-sleeved white blouse with a full black skirt, as was Mother's custom. The children encountered the apparition of an older man in the basement, and when they told it to go away, it promptly disappeared. Experts think this could have been Otto or the bachelor, Merrill Henry, who puttered around and often helped Otto with the building's upkeep and repairs. Occasionally, an apparition that resembles Otto has been seen with a wispy-looking Mother Bross standing in the second-floor hall.

Hotchkiss Paranormal investigated the activity at the hotel in the summer of 2014, and Hector, the group's leader, spent the night in room 2. Sometime during the night, he awoke to feel invisible hands gently tucking the covers around him, even making sure his feet were well covered. Other members of this group caught glimpses of both Mother Bross and WT during the night.

When another team of investigators visited the hotel, their electromagnetic field meter (EMF) recorded high readings in the dining room near the antique mirror. The batteries on their two cameras and also their video camera were immediately drained when they entered room 2. They obtained high readings on their EMF meter, and the spirit box picked up many strange sounds. When they asked several questions, hoping the spirit box would pick up an answer, they didn't get any replies. When they started their investigation in room 2, they placed their equipment on the bed and then straightened the bedspread when finished before leaving. When they returned to the room a few minutes later, they were surprised to see that the bedspread was rumpled as if someone had been sitting on the bed.

16
CRESTED BUTTE

Crested Butte, Colorado's last great ski town, has been spared the development that transformed the rugged mining camps of Telluride and Aspen into glitzy resorts. Crested Butte wasn't a silver or gold boom town; its wealth was in coal. Many who call it home today are descendants of immigrants from Italy, Slovenia, Croatia, or Cornwall. Their ancestors came by the shipload, eager to get a job in the coal mines. They built homes, churches, and a school and raised their families here. Today, their descendants are fiercely protective of their roots, which are deeply entwined in Crested Butte's history.

Regarded as a preservation pacesetter in Colorado, Crested Butte received History Colorado's Stephen H. Hart Award for the restoration of its numerous historic structures. In 1974, this entire town of nineteenth-century Victorian buildings was designated as the Crested Butte National Historic District.

Around 1861, eager prospectors who'd come west in the Pike's Peak gold rush made their way into this part of the Elk Mountains, where they found about $1 million worth of gold dust and nuggets in the icy streams. Their intrusion infuriated the Utes, and as the gold began to run out, the prospectors, fearing attack, fled from the mountains.

The Utes controlled the Elk Mountains until the prospectors returned in the 1870s, armed with new maps of the region that had been prepared by the Hayden Geologic survey of 1873–74. Daring prospectors, who ventured far into the Elk Mountains, discovered silver on the high peaks and started the new mining camps of Gothic, Irwin, and Ruby. The Hayden surveyors had named two of the area's prominent peaks, Gothic Mountain and Mount Crested Butte.

In 1877, entrepreneur Howard Smith planned a town in the valley at the base of Mount Crested Butte. It would become a supply center for prospectors in the silver camps in the nearby mountains. Smith built a sawmill to provide lumber for new buildings and a smelter to process silver ore. Taking the name of the neighboring mountain, Smith organized the Crested Butte Town Company, laid out a town site, and began selling lots on July 3, 1880. Prices quickly escalated from $35 to $750 a lot after representatives of the Denver & Rio Grande Railroad snatched up much of the land, accumulating one-half interest in the budding town.

The railroad men wanted to haul silver ore from the new mines to the smelters, but they also coveted the real treasure of Crested Butte— its enormous deposits of coal. Great layers of bituminous coal had been discovered just west of Crested Butte, as well as some veins of hard anthracite coal. This turned out to be the only deposit of anthracite coal west of Pennsylvania, and it was quite valuable. Colorado Coal and Iron Company opened its Jokerville Mine on Coal Creek in 1880. This company would eventually become the Colorado Fuel and Iron Company (CF&I) and dominate the coal industry in the Rocky Mountains. Men who'd worked in the coal mines of Pennsylvania and West Virginia came west, looking for jobs in Crested Butte's mines. They were joined by immigrants from the British Isles and northern Europe, Greece, Italy, and the Slavic countries of southern Europe. Experienced coal miners, they brought their families and gave Crested Butte a solid foundation that was so different from Colorado's boom-and-bust mining camps.

The D&RG rushed to lay its narrow-gauge tracks up the valley from Gunnison, arriving in Crested Butte on November 24, 1881. As soon as the new depot had been completed, one of the first trains to chug out of town was pulling three boxcars and thirteen carloads of coal to heat homes in chilly Gunnison.

Crested Butte grew rapidly as a supply center after the D&RG arrived, bringing reasonably priced food, goods, materials, and equipment for the town and the mining camps. The main street, Elk Avenue, was usually dusty and crowded with freight wagons and long strings of mules and burro pack trains loading goods to be hauled to the mines. This commerce ended with the first snowfall, which closed the treacherous trails over the passes, blocking them with drifts that piled up as deep as fifteen feet. The railroad could only run regularly to Crested Butte from July to January due to the heavy winter snows.

In the mountains west of Crested Butte in the late fall of 1879, a prospector named Fisher found deposits of ruby silver ore, a silver-bearing mineral with deep-red crystals. He made two claims, the "Forest Queen" and the "Ruby Chief," and sent ore samples to Denver to be smelted and assayed. Fisher's ore proved to be high-quality silver, and news of his rich find spread through Denver long before he received the news. By spring, thousands of hopefuls were flooding this new silver field in the Elk Mountains.

By 1880, the Ruby Mining District was organized, and a small camp called "Ruby City" was established. When winter approached, several prospectors decided to stay, despite the bitter cold and howling blizzards that filled their prospecting holes with snow. Overwhelming drifts completely buried their cabins, forcing them to shovel tunnels from their cabin doors up to the surface of the snow. When a party of miners traveling on snowshoes arrived in early spring, they looked around but couldn't find Ruby City or see any cabins. Eventually, they noticed plumes of smoke drifting up through holes in the snow—vents for the chimneys of cabins hidden deep beneath.

By 1882, Crested Butte had one thousand residents, a bank, a newspaper, several saloons and restaurants, three livery stables, and a church. The arrival of the railroad brought reasonable prices for supplies and fueled continued growth. Freight for the silver towns of Aspen and Ashcroft came by rail to Crested Butte and was carried by burro pack trains over treacherous Pearl Pass.

Most of the town's saloons were along Elk Avenue and Second Street, and after their shifts, coal miners often stopped in for a drink or two at the Croatian Hall, the Elk Bar, Spritzer's Bar, the Slogar Bar, or the Bucket of Blood. Crested Butte had a small red-light district of three or four buildings near the saloons, but unlike some Colorado mining towns, the madams had no role in the social or business scene.

In 1882, the first fifty coke ovens were built at the Jokerville Mine, which supplied coal to Leadville, Pueblo, and Denver. Within a year, three anthracite mines, three bituminous coal mines, and 150 coke ovens were in operation there. The Jokerville Mine was the pride of CF&I, steadily producing bituminous coal. It was a very dangerous mine because of "firedamp," which are the flammable gases, particularly methane, that build up in the coal itself. These highly poisonous, flammable gases can't be seen or smelled, but they suddenly explode. Coal dust and the naked flame head lamps that were used by miners to light their way through the tunnels greatly increased this danger of explosions.

On January 24, 1884, a thunderous explosion at the Jokerville Mine killed fifty-nine men, including two twelve-year-old gatekeepers. Almost every family in town lost at least one relative, and flags were flown at half-mast everywhere. The miners were buried together in one mass grave with a single marker in the Crested Butte Cemetery. The Jokerville Mine was closed, but that same year, CF&I opened another coal mine, called the Big Mine, and built 150 additional coke ovens. CF&I was Crested Butte's largest employer, and by 1902, the Big Mine was producing one thousand tons of coal a day.

Most of Crested Butte's buildings were wood frame construction, and the first catastrophic fire came on January 25, 1890. It destroyed most of the business district, and the poorly equipped volunteer firemen were reduced to throwing snow on the out-of-control flames. Unlike many towns that rebuilt with bricks and stone after a fire, Crested Butte again used lumber.

In January 1893, there was another fire. Once again, it destroyed most of the business district. This time, the water lines were frozen, and as they tried to remove fuel sources from the advancing flames, the firemen's overenthusiastic dynamiting destroyed several uninsured commercial buildings and blew a gaping hole in the side of city hall. Once again, rebuilding was done with lumber. There were more fires in 1899 and in 1901, and this time the firemen couldn't douse the flames because they had no fire hoses. Crested Butte rebuilt—with wood.

The 1893 repeal of the Sherman Silver Purchase Act ended Colorado's silver boom and closed the smelters, decreasing the need for coal. Coal miners had been working for low wages, sometimes earning as little as one dollar a day, and their working conditions were very dangerous. Corrupt mine management easily took advantage of the immigrant workers, who often spoke no English. In 1895, the company store arrived in Crested Butte, making the coal miners' financial situation even more difficult. Instead of paying their employees in cash, the mine owners switched to scrip, which could only be exchanged for its face value in the company store. The miners' wives had to pay inflated company prices for their food, clothing, and supplies. This returned a tidy profit to the company, and the miners grew resentful. Unions protested loudly about this practice, and by 1899, CF&I had received a lot of bad publicity because of this practice.

There was a great deal of unrest among CF&I's coal miners, and as the eastern labor unions gained members, there were several violent strikes in the early twentieth century. The International Workers of the World (the Wobblies) and the Ku Klux Klan tried to recruit coal miners in Crested Butte, but they had little success among the immigrant workers.

Prohibition began early in Colorado in 1916, but Crested Butte never went completely dry. Saloons were converted into soda fountains that continued to serve homemade wine, white lightning, and bathtub gin. The advent of the automobile was a great boon to the bootleggers, and the revenue agents who came to town had little luck finding their stills. In October 1927, the town's newspaper, the *Pilot*, was indignant when the "Feds" arrested nine "of our most prominent bootleggers" and destroyed a few stills. The paper insisted "someone had tipped off" the revenue agents.

After World War I, Crested Butte's coal production decreased as CF&I developed new mines closer to the steel mills in Pueblo. During the late 1930s and 1940s, the mines began laying off workers, and some of the smaller coal mines closed. In 1952, the Big Mine shut down operations, and with no coal to haul, the Denver & Rio Grande shut down the rail line to Crested Butte. This ended the era of coal and left Crested Butte facing hard times. Many people left town searching for work on local ranches or in the coke ovens and mills in Pueblo and Denver.

The mood in town wavered between despair and resignation, but the air was finally clear. For years, Crested Butte had crouched beneath clouds of dense, black smoke and soot from the coke ovens, but now the mountains and blue skies could be seen once again. In 1963, a fledgling ski resort, Crested Butte Limited, opened, and today thousands come for winter sports on Mount Crested Butte. In the summer, visitors come to see hillsides that are a riot of color in this legislature-designated "Wildflower Capital of Colorado." Locals are proud of their tiny town and often brag, "Crested Butte, like Aspen once was!"

Forest Queen Hotel

The picturesque Forest Queen Hotel, with its high, wooden false front, hunkers down in its historic spot on Elk Avenue, where it was built in 1882. The two-story frame structure is the town's oldest hotel and looks much as it did a century ago. Plenty of drinks were served at the old wooden bar in the first-floor restaurant, the Coal Creek Grill, which replaced the rowdy saloon.

One of the town's original buildings, the Forest Queen escaped the numerous fires that destroyed most of the business district. It was first a hotel-bar combination, but then the owner decided a bar with a brothel

The Forest Queen, built in 1882, is one of Crested Butte's oldest buildings. *Courtesy of Wendy Williams.*

upstairs would be more profitable. One-Eye Ruby, who came by her name honestly, ran the Forest Queen with an iron hand for years.

The stories about the ghosts of the Forest Queen didn't trouble Barry Cornman when he bought the hotel in the early twentieth century. He and his mother, Thelma, operated it successfully for years, although Thelma was unpopular in Crested Butte. She was quite bossy and irritated the employees and miners who boarded there. This imperious, pushy woman barked and yelled orders at everyone and was often called the "Queen of the Forest Queen." When Prohibition was approved in Colorado in 1916, it sounded the death knell for most saloons, but Cornman held on until 1919, when he finally closed his profitable business.

In 1920, young Yugoslavian immigrants Mike and Katherine Perko purchased the old hotel-bar and converted it into a general store. The grocery was on the first floor, and the Perkos lived upstairs. Their family grew rapidly, and the Perkos had plenty of help as their eight children sorted vegetables, swept the floors, and manned the cash register.

When Mike Perko died in 1949, he was buried in the Crested Butte Cemetery. His grieving wife, Katherine, died just a year later. Their children, once grown, sold the building in 1958 to Dr. Hubert Smith, a lawyer-physician who founded the Law Science Academy in Crested Butte. The old hotel-grocery and several houses around town were used as lodging for participants who came to study with Dr. Smith. The Forest Queen was dubbed the Academy Arms during this period, and Dr. Smith envisioned intellectual gatherings similar to those held at the Aspen Institute. In 1971, Dr. Smith's idealistic venture flopped, the academy folded, and the hotel was empty, left to its memories and ghosts.

Ghosts

Sometime during the late 1800s, Elizabeth, nicknamed Liz, joined Ruby's crew of working girls. She was a pretty woman who laughed a lot, and she became a favorite of the miners. Then a roaming gambler came to town and made the Forest Queen his headquarters. The handsome charmer captivated Liz and promised to whisk her away to the big-city life in Denver. She shared her romantic hopes with the other girls and refused to heed their warnings about double-dealing men.

The lovestruck couple needed money to make their dreams come true so the gambler charmed Liz into loaning him every penny she'd saved. Flush with Liz's money, the gambler bought into a high-stakes card game and won piles of cash. Then he sneaked out of town with all the winnings—alone. Poor Liz was devastated when she learned that her handsome gambler was really gone, leaving her alone and penniless. Every day, she sank deeper into depression, staying in her room and drinking too much. The miners missed her laughter and bright smile, but she refused all their entreaties to join them. Then one cold wintry night, Liz could bear it no longer and jumped out of a second-story window to her death.

The melancholy spirit of Liz hangs around the Forest Queen, sometimes waking guests as she bangs and slams doors at night. After an especially noisy night, a disheveled guest dashed down the stairs, yelling, "I'm getting out of here! Nobody can get any sleep here!" Liz often sets the kitchen on its ear, tossing pots and pans about and loudly rattling through the cupboards. Occasionally, large cooking utensils disappear from the kitchen, turning up later in odd places.

A prostitute named Liz committed suicide by jumping from the second-story window of the Forest Queen. *Courtesy of Wendy Williams.*

Room 4 has a lot of nocturnal activity, and a guest in room 1 insisted that he saw the apparition of a strange woman wandering about his room. His personal items were moved around, his keys disappeared, and the lights kept flickering on and off much of the night. The doors of a room may slam open suddenly, startling the person inside. When you go to look in the hall, there's never anyone around. The housekeeping staff often finds the beds in vacant rooms rumpled and wrinkled as if someone had slept there. Once when a chef stayed overnight in the hotel's only two-bed room, he awoke in the morning to find that all of his clothes had been laid out on the other bed.

Liz is sometimes called the Red Lady Ghost, and she could be responsible for the electrical disturbances that occur in the hotel and restaurant, especially in the restrooms. One man entered the bathroom, and the lights went out—at the same time, his cellphone was knocked forcefully from his hand. There was no one else in the bathroom. This has occurred several times in the men's restroom. Employees who are working alone at night often say they feel like they are being watched.

Crested Butte was once a tough coal mining town, whose residents hung on through hard times, and some still remain behind. The town is full of tales of ghosts of miners who died in the Jokerville tragedy and other mine disasters. Others were swept away by sudden avalanches, and locals warn about ghostly strangers wandering along the roads and near the cemetery.

17
CRIPPLE CREEK

Cripple Creek was the scene of Colorado's last gold rush, and it ended the economic depression of 1893 when 50 percent of the men were unemployed. Cowboy Bob Womack's discovery of unlikely looking gray rocks near a creek where a cow broke her leg started a boom that produced millions of dollars' worth of gold.

Womack drank too much, and nobody would loan him money to develop his new claim. He put a few samples of this gray rock in a window of a Colorado Springs furniture store, hoping to attract an investor. A sharp-eyed, self-taught geologist recognized these samples as a complex mineral that combines with gold or silver. He learned the location of Womack's claim and hurried to stake his own claim nearby. Next, he marked off a six-square-mile area around Womack's discovery, named it the Cripple Creek Mining District, and set to work.

Womack woke up one morning to realize that in a drunken stupor he'd sold his claim for a paltry $500. When developed, it became the Gold King Mine, which produced $5 million in gold. Womack made more potentially rich claims, but he always sold them before trying to mine any. He celebrated the sale of one claim on Christmas Day 1893 by passing out $1 bills to children in front of his favorite saloon. In 1909, Bob Womack died in Colorado Springs without a penny.

It's ironic that much of Cripple Creek's gold was found in a ten-square-mile area where many rich discoveries were made by dentists, firemen, teachers, and clerks who knew nothing about prospecting. A pharmacist, who had no idea where to look for gold, tossed his hat into the air and started digging where it landed. He hit a rich vein, which became the Pharmacist Mine, making him one of the district's first millionaires.

Prospectors Pat and Mike were down to their last dollar and decided they'd dig at the next spot their dog lifted his leg. The pup stopped, and they dug and struck a wide band of gold, which became the wealthy Last Dollar Mine.

Realtors Horace Bennett and Julius Myers bought 640 acres, platted a town site, named the principal streets after themselves, sold lots, and made a quick million dollars. They called the new town "Fremont." After just two months, there were eight hundred people living in tents, cabins, and shacks scattered around Fremont. When the town was awarded a post office, the government changed the name Fremont to "Cripple Creek."

In addition to hopeful prospectors, hordes of hustlers, gamblers, and con men—scheming to grab a share of the golden fortune—headed for Cripple Creek. Soon there was an abundance of saloons, brothels, and dance halls lining Myers Avenue, the red-light district. Prostitutes were banned from plying their trade on Bennett Avenue, the business boulevard of banks, brokerage houses, and hotels. By 1894, there were ten thousand people in Cripple Creek, with five hundred more arriving every month.

The year 1894 brought the first labor strike. Miners worked ten hours for less than three dollars a day, and their working conditions were deplorable. Injuries and deaths from explosions, falls, cave-ins, poisonous fumes, and falling rocks were common. The loss of an arm or leg or having one's head blown off was a daily risk for them, and there was no compensation for families when an accident happened. Miners joined the union of the Western Federation of Mine Workers (WFM) for support. When their demands for an eight-hour day for three-dollar wages were denied by mine owners, they went on strike.

Winfield Stratton, who'd become Cripple Creek's first millionaire, remembered his hungry times as a prospector and met the union's demands at his Independence Mine. His hopes that other mine owners would follow his example were dashed, and tensions between labor and management escalated into violence and mayhem. There were gunfights, buildings were dynamited, two men were killed, and the state militia came twice to establish order in Cripple Creek. The miners' strike lasted five months, and the union finally won an eight-hour workday for a wage of three dollars.

Railroad tracks were gradually replacing the rough stage roads to Cripple Creek, and the Florence & Cripple Creek Railroad (F&CC), financed by the

Denver & Rio Grande, was the first to steam into town on July 1, 1894. The entire population turned out to cheer and celebrate, and in December 1894, the Colorado Midland Railroad arrived. Now two railroads were busily hauling gold ore to the smelters from mines in this area. Spur lines were built to the two dozen satellite towns and their mines scattered through the surrounding hills. The Cripple Creek Mining District eventually produced more millions of dollars in gold than California did in the 1849 gold rush.

Disaster struck on the morning of April 25, 1896, when a scuffle between a bartender and his girlfriend tipped over a stove, starting a fire. Fanned by strong winds, the flames took off, destroying most of the Myers Avenue red-light district. Then it blew toward the business district, consuming banks, shops, and the post office with its twenty-five thousand pieces of mail. Within three hours, Cripple Creek suffered over $1 million in damages, two lives were lost, and 3,600 people were homeless.

Just three days later on April 29, a pot of grease caught fire in a hotel kitchen, and the flames exploded into a raging inferno. The April 30, 1896 *Rocky Mountain News* reported that "the whole city rushed to the scene, dropping tools from their hands. The fire jumped with a roar like a hungry giant at his prey. Floods of water and the demolition of buildings with deafening explosions of dynamite didn't stop the fire, and men stood with tears running down their cheeks, helpless." Terrified people piled their

In April 1896, Cripple Creek endured two disastrous fires within a period of ninety-six hours. *Courtesy of History Colorado.*

children, pets, and possessions into wagons and rushed to leave the burning town. The fire roared through fifteen blocks of businesses, destroying four hundred buildings, and leaving six thousand people homeless.

When word of this disaster reached millionaire Winfield Stratton, he quickly formed a relief committee; volunteers collected tents, thousands of blankets, and diapers. Stratton loaded the supplies on a two-car train in Colorado Springs, and it headed for Cripple Creek, stopping at towns along the route to pick up more donations. When the supply train whistled into Cripple Creek late on April 29, it was greeted with thankful cheers and plenty of grateful tears. The supplies were distributed among the bedraggled, sooty citizens, many of whom had lost everything. Stratton organized a second relief train carrying food, which volunteers rushed to gather, taking everything from canned vegetables, cases of canned beef, beans, condensed milk, and crackers, to every loaf of bread in town. They tucked in jelly and preserves, liquor, and piles of cooking pots. When the food train arrived at dawn in Cripple Creek, it was met by grateful, hungry people who cheered and cried as the food was distributed.

Cripple Creek was soon clearing the disaster debris, and the city council passed an ordinance requiring all new commercial buildings to be built of brick. Most of the handsome new brick and stone buildings were decorated with rosettes, stained-glass windows, cast-iron pillars, and dated 1896. Six months after the fires, the population had increased by ten thousand. By 1900, Cripple Creek was Colorado's fourth-largest city, with a population of twenty-five thousand. At its height, the mining district's population peaked at fifty thousand. Over five hundred mines had produced more than $18 million in gold by 1900, and the mining district's total production was well over $77 million. Cripple Creek and Victor boasted twenty-eight millionaires and countless others who'd become incredibly wealthy.

Another labor strike in 1903–4 lasted fifteen months, and it was one of the bloodiest and most violent in Colorado's history. Governor Peabody called out the National Guard and declared martial law in Cripple Creek. Over two hundred union members were rounded up, loaded on trains, dumped across the state line, and forbidden to return. Mine owners banned organized labor in the Cripple Creek Mining District, and gold production was cut in half, scaring off investors and damaging the mine owners financially.

In 1906, Carrie Nation, called the "hatchet-face mascot of the WCTU" (Woman's Christian Temperance Union), who specialized in invading saloons and chopping bars into pieces with her hatchet, came to Cripple Creek. As she marched up Bennett Avenue, leading a parade of temperance sympathizers, doors of liquor emporiums were slammed in her face. When she discovered Johnny Nolan's Saloon was open, she stomped in, axe raised. When she saw Nolan's prize, the Botticelli painting of a nude, *Birth of Venus*, she screamed, "Hang a blanket over that trollop! If that naked witch isn't covered up, I'll chop her to shreds!" She charged at the painting, hatchet raised, and began slashing at it. Nolan grabbed her, spun her around, and knocked the axe from her hands. The sheriff speedily hauled Carrie off to jail, where she spent the night cooling off. In the morning, Nolan himself bailed her out and loaded her on the train for Colorado Springs. Always a gentleman, Johnny Nolan politely advised Carrie not to return to Cripple Creek.

By 1910, the price of gold was falling, and water was seeping into the deep mine tunnels from underground streams. Pumps could not clear the tunnels, and as workers drilled deeper than eight hundred feet, the water flow increased. Large tunnels were built at great expense to drain off the water, but the flooding continued. During World War II, the government ordered all mines that weren't producing copper, lead, or zinc for the war effort to close. Only a few gold mines were able to resume operations after the war ended, and most shut down permanently in the 1950s.

Descendants of burros that worked in the mines roam Cripple Creek's streets. *Courtesy of Tom Williams.*

Cripple Creek's population dropped to a few hundred people, who began joking that their four-legged population was larger than the two-legged one. When the mines closed, the little burros that had pulled ore carts and wagons and carried supplies and equipment were out of work, just like the miners. Turned loose to roam the streets, they demolished gardens, tipped over garbage cans, and begged for handouts. They became children's pets and hung around posing for pictures with tourists. They still wander around town. In 1931, crowds poured into Cripple Creek for the first Donkey Derby Days, and this popular event has taken place every summer since. All proceeds go to the Two Mile High Club for the care and feeding of Cripple Creek's burros.

In 1990, Colorado voters approved limited-stakes gambling in Cripple Creek, Black Hawk, and Central City, and their old buildings had facelifts before becoming casinos. Gold mining resumed at the Cripple Creek & Victor Gold Mine, an open pit mine where gold is recovered by heap leaching. This mine is now the largest gold producer in Colorado.

Imperial Hotel

After the ashes of the devastating 1896 fires cooled, construction of the three-story brick Imperial Hotel was started, and it was completed before the end of the year. The hotel was leased by a widow, Mrs. E.F. Collins, who called it the Collins Hotel. She rented rooms to mining engineers, stockbrokers, assayers, and professional men for three dollars per day, with meals included.

In 1906, a Mrs. Shoot took over the business, renaming it the New Collins Hotel. She annexed the three-story building next door and connected the two structures with an elevated passageway. This hotel had seventy rooms with steam heat, electric lights, private bathrooms, and a large dining room, which could seat three hundred. Many elegant dinners and soirees attended by gilt-edged guests from England, Wales, and France were held at the hotel, and the society columns were filled with news of club socials, ladies' luncheons, and elaborate teas hosted at the New Collins. Despite the hotel's popularity, Mrs. Shoot fell behind on her mortgage payments, and George Long, who held her note, foreclosed in 1910.

Long was a wealthy English aristocrat who'd come to America to escape the gossip after he married his first cousin Ursula. A descendant of royalty,

The Imperial Hotel was built in 1896 after two disastrous fires destroyed much of Cripple Creek. *Courtesy of History Colorado.*

George received a monthly stipend from the British Crown, which enabled his family to live very comfortably. George and Ursula renovated the hotel and converted it into a stylish Victorian establishment, changed the name to the Imperial Hotel, and ordered expensive new furniture.

The Longs lived in an apartment in the hotel with their young son, Stephen, and daughter, Alice, who was mentally ill. She had tantrums and flew into rages so violent that the Longs were forced to lock her in the apartment alone when they had hotel responsibilities. George Long was described as a shy, "gentle wispy man," whose hearing was impaired, and he preferred to putter around in his basement shop while his wife entertained their guests.

The Longs' fleet of seven shiny Pierce Arrow limousines, driven by smartly liveried drivers, met the train from Colorado Springs every day. They welcomed travelers and drove them to the Imperial, where as many as three hundred were served a fine luncheon with plenty of wine in the spacious dining room. Then everyone clambered aboard the train for the trip back down the mountain to Colorado Springs.

In 1940, George died from a fall down the basement stairs, and when the accident was investigated, it turned out to be murder. An angry Alice had walloped George in the head with an iron skillet when he was coming up the stairs. Then she pushed him, causing his fatal fall backward down the steps. Alice spent the rest of her life in a mental institution for the crime.

Ursula Long was heartbroken by her husband's death, but she managed to keep the hotel open for four more years and then gave up. The Imperial sat vacant and neglected for decades until Wayne and Dorothy Mackin purchased it in 1946. This optimistic young couple saw potential in the dismal, down-at-the-heels building, sitting crookedly on its steep hillside lot. The fine furnishings were gone, and the only things left in the faded lobby were an old potbellied stove and a scuffed roll-top desk.

The Mackins began a room-by-room renovation: scrubbing away accumulated grime, scraping off old paint, removing stained, peeling wallpaper, refinishing and polishing the hardwood floors, and renovating the kitchen. They remodeled the owners' apartment, bought cheap furniture at auctions, and moved in. By the summer of 1947, the kitchen was functional, and the dining room was ready for customers. Their hard work paid off, and the Imperial soon gained a reputation for serving good food

Imperial Hotel hosted the longest-running melodrama theater in the nation. *Courtesy of Tom Williams.*

In 1947, the Mackins presented the first performances of an old-fashioned melodrama, which received rave reviews. They hired a troupe of traveling performers and converted the basement into a cabaret-style theater, called the Gold Bar Room Theater. In 1953, they opened ta luxurious lounge in the Red Rooster Room and introduced the new Imperial Players as permanent performers. By 1996, their renowned productions had become the nation's longest-running melodrama theater. The Mackins' son, Stephen, took over management of the hotel in the 1980s and continued its operation until the Imperial was sold in 1991. After Colorado voters approved legalized gambling, the hotel underwent several ownership changes and subsequent renovations.

Ghosts

The ghost of George Long, who loved the Imperial, might be responsible for the mysterious activity in the hotel's casino. A night-shift casino employee named Richard Duwe was startled when a slot machine suddenly began dumping out coins. The casino was closed, and no one was around. Security cameras showed that one slot machine spitting out hundreds of dollars in coins—although all the slots have a variety of mechanisms to prevent this. The Colorado Gaming Commission examined the machine and found no evidence of tampering or malfunctioning, leaving many to wonder if George had been tinkering around.

On another night, after the casino closed, quiet and empty, Duwe heard the familiar "ding" of a coin dropping into a slot machine. He radioed security, thinking that a customer had managed to stay after closing, hidden, and now was trying his luck. Duwe and the security officer searched the entire casino and found no one. None of the slots had its "Coin Accepted" light on. The security officer settled the question, saying, "It was probably just George!" Duwe became convinced that there was a ghost sharing his night shift at the Imperial,

Several people who have abilities as a medium have picked up the presence of various spirits in the hotel, and these "sensitives" have noticed there are different levels of both negative and positive energy present in different areas. The old lobby has been restored and looks just like it did over one hundred years ago, but most guests don't linger here, saying they feel like they're being watched. Others may get a "creepy" feeling on the stairs where George Long fell to his death, and still more say they sense a presence downstairs. Employees have seen shadowy figures and felt mysterious touches. Remodeling often stirs up resident spirits, and several paranormal investigators commented that one entity was very angry about the presence of so many people in the hotel casino.

There are unexplained loud banging sounds, and employees have heard scratching sounds at the door to the Red Rooster Bar—as if someone was trying to get it open. This was once the apartment where the Longs locked Alice when she became violent. Rick Wood, who formerly led the Cripple Creek Ghost Walk Tours, said that George often wandered about the halls of the Imperial and that he was especially active in rooms 39 and 42. The water faucets was often turned on and left running in these bathroom sinks, and the doors opened and closed by themselves. Through the years, George has been blamed for jammed dresser drawers, stereos that don't work, and doors slamming unexpectedly. Wood said that George was always blamed if a woman's behind was discreetly patted. One man who stayed at the hotel said he spent a restless night and kept waking up. In the early morning hours, he said, "I woke up and thought I saw a man in a straw hat and white shirt standing by my bed. I guess I was dreaming, but it sure seemed real."

Jeff Belanger, author of the book *The World's Most Haunted Places*, interviewed Stephen Mackin, who spent the first seven years of his life in the apartment—now the Red Rooster. Stephen said his family never publicized the hotel's ghost, although they were aware of its presence and referred to it as "the silent owner.'" Mackin said, "I'm sure that George is still there somehow. Nobody in my immediate family ever saw him, but I had a director for my theater who saw him. I also had a couple of actors who saw him." He continued, "A couple of people who worked in the kitchen also saw him." He explained, "The things that we did see from George were all friendly things. There was nothing spooky or evil or anything like that." One actor who saw George standing behind the bar downstairs recalled "a well-dressed man with a balding head with a thin ring of 'monk-like hair.'" That fits George's description perfectly.

St. Nicholas Hotel

By 1893, Cripple Creek had eighty practicing physicians but no hospital. The town's citizens appealed to the Sisters of Mercy to open a facility to care for the sick and injured. They even offered to donate wooden frame house that could serve as a small hospital. On January 4, 1894, the Sisters of Mercy opened St. Nicholas Hospital in the donated house, and they treated three hundred patients the first year.

In April 1896, when flames from two disastrous fires almost destroyed Cripple Creek, the nuns hurried to evacuate the hospital and move their patients to safety. While the nuns were working frantically, a member of an anti-Catholic group sneaked into the hospital's kitchen and planted dynamite in the stove's chimney. He wanted to totally destroy the nuns' hospital, but his evil plan backfired when the dynamite suddenly exploded and blew off his leg. The merciful sisters treated his injury and calmly evacuated him with the rest of their patients. Cripple Creek's disastrous fires left thousands homeless in cold weather, but luckily, the hospital was spared. After the flames were subdued, the nuns brought their patients back to their little house. They were surprised to find the dynamiter's leg, minus his shoe, which had been blown off and landed in their tea kettle.

As Victor, Cripple Creek, and their satellite mining communities grew, the nuns bought land on a hill overlooking Cripple Creek and hired a Denver architect to design a state-of-the-art hospital. When it was completed, the three-story brick building had steam heat with hot and cold running water, electricity, and a modern surgery department with an operating room. St. Nicholas Hospital had twenty-six patient rooms, one of which was elegantly

The St. Nicholas Hotel was once a hospital, opened in 1898 by the Sisters of Mercy. *Courtesy of Tom Williams.*

furnished by mine owner Bert Carlton to be used by his ill or injured employees. Eventually, a small ward was added for the mentally ill. The nuns lived on the third floor, while the orderlies' quarters were in the attic above. The huge boiler in the basement kept the place toasty in the winter, although it used over one hundred pounds of coal a day.

The hospital opened in March 1898, and the first patient was a miner who'd had an unfortunate fall down a mine shaft. During a smallpox epidemic in 1901, the nuns vaccinated as many as possible and cared for all of the sick. During the 1918 Spanish influenza pandemic, the hospital was inundated with deathly ill patients, and so many people died that bodies were piled outside the funeral home. In 1925, the nuns sold St. Nicholas to a group of physicians, who operated it as a private hospital. It remained open until 1960, when the county bought it for one dollar.

In 1972, the hospital closed and sat vacant for years until it was purchased in 1995. It was remodeled into a hotel with fifteen Victorian-style rooms, all with private baths. The massive safe in the office that was manufactured around 1900 has been in use for over one hundred years. Numerous photos of the hospital's early days are displayed throughout the hotel, and there are sweeping views of Cripple Creek, its mines, and the Sangre de Cristo Mountains.

Ghosts

Spirits of some long-departed patients and a few dedicated nuns drift around the St. Nicholas, but Stinky can't be missed. A foul odor around the hospital's back stairs is a tip-off, and occasionally, someone catches a glimpse of a worn-looking miner. Sometimes only half of the miner's body is seen floating down these back stairs. There are many stories about Petey, an orphan, who lived at the hospital and was taken care of by the nuns. He's a mischievous spirit and is often seen darting around the hotel. His favorite spot is the tiny Boiler Room Tavern, where he moves bottles around, hides keys, and creates small disturbances.

When the hotel owner was working in the small office behind the old cashier's booth in the lobby, she was startled by a strange sound. Looking around, she saw a tall, thin man in a long coat and wearing a derby. He just looked at her and then vanished. Another employee was frightened when she saw this thin man, similarly dressed, pass by her and slowly disappear

Patient rooms have been renovated into comfortable guest rooms. *Courtesy of Tom Williams.*

while she watched. A group of six men were standing at the small tavern bar talking when the doorbell rang. When one of the men answered the door, no one was there. He said he felt something touch his shoulder, and he turned to see a tall, shadowy figure walk past him and right through the back wall.

Guests in room 11, which was once the hospital's operating room, have been awakened by the sound of crying. They've seen a little girl standing at the foot of their bed, and then she vanishes. Guests have been awakened by children laughing and the sounds of a ball bouncing about on the third floor. This paranormal activity has occurred when there are no young children staying at the hotel.

The St. Nicholas Hotel has been investigated by several paranormal groups, including Southwest Paranormal and Spirit Chasers. Their observations and video recordings can be seen on the internet. Another group of investigators from Digital Dowsing and Darkness Radio spent three days tracking the spirits at this old hospital. They obtained some interesting EVPs and a video that can be seen on the internet.

18

VICTOR

Winfield Scott Stratton could not believe his luck. He'd prospected all over Colorado since 1872, living on beans and hope. In 1891, he'd found some promising rocks on Battle Mountain and staked a claim, naming it the Independence, since he'd found it on the holiday. Stratton worked this claim sporadically for two years but discovered only a little gold. Disgusted, he decided to sell the worthless Independence in 1893, but the night before he was to finalize the sale, he accidentally discovered a rich vein of gold in a side tunnel. He estimated it would yield at least $1million in gold ore. Stratton carefully concealed the vein and spent a restless night worrying over a way to get out of the sale. The next day, the prospective buyer complained about the claim's poor potential and asked if he could cancel their deal and get out of the purchase. Stratton could hardly believe his luck and readily agreed. He began working the Independence mine in earnest, and within just six months, Stratton was the mining district's first millionaire.

Battle Mountain was overrun with prospectors when Frank and Harry Woods arrived from Illinois. They formed an investment company with their father and snapped up 136 acres at the foot of the mountain. They platted a town site, named it Victor, and began selling lots, claiming each would be a "gold mine." Lots were quickly grabbed, and wood frame saloons, restaurants, stores, and homes were soon being hammered together.

The richest gold mines in the Cripple Creek Mining District—the Independence, the Portland, and the Ajax Mines—were all located on

The headframe of William Stratton's Independence gold mine on Battle Mountain. *Courtesy of Tom Williams.*

Battle Mountain. The steady stream of gold they produced helped Colorado recover from the terrible economic depression that followed the 1893 repeal of the Sherman Silver Purchase Act. Cripple Creek became a rich man's town and was the social, financial, and political center of the mining district. Victor was known as "The City of Mines." It was a working man's town, the center of the rail and shipping district, and the home of the labor force that worked in the district's five-hundred-plus gold mines.

    Miners and their families lived in boardinghouses or clapboard and brick homes that crouched in the shadows of Battle Mountain's skeletal head-frames and towering mine dumps. Daily underground blasts set the windows to rattling, and the dishes clattered as heavy ore wagons rumbled through the streets. Both the Florence & Cripple Creek Railroad and the Colorado Midland Railroad arrived in Victor in 1894. Just two years later, the population was around eighteen thousand, and there was an old saying that began, "Cripple Creek gets the glory, but Victor has the gold."

The Woods boys completed their Victor Hotel and then founded the First National Bank, which was situated on the ground floor. Then they started the Pike's Peak Power Company, the forerunner of today's Southern Colorado Power Company. It supplied hydroelectric power to Victor, Cripple Creek, and even Pueblo.

Disaster struck on August 21, 1899, when a fire began in a Paradise Alley brothel. Within a few hours, the blazing inferno had consumed fourteen city blocks and about eight hundred buildings. Victor was destroyed—just a pile of ashes. There was $1.5 million in damages, and 1,500 people were homeless. The Woods brothers, the town's largest property holders, suffered huge losses.

Victor's citizens began rebuilding with bricks and stone, and within a few days, restaurants, shops, and saloons were back in business. The Woods brothers built the new four-story brick Victor Hotel and opened their First National Bank of Victor on the ground floor. Then they rebuilt the Gold Coin Club, an elegant clubhouse with a bowling alley, gymnasium, and library for their miners and other employees.

The Victor Hotel opened in 1900 and is in the National Register of Historic Places. *Courtesy of History Colorado, Fred Mazzulla Collection.*

Around the turn of the century, the eighteen thousand people living in Victor and the surrounding towns were served by three competing railroads. Railroad cars carrying gold ore headed down the mountains every day to the huge smelter at Colorado City and returned with their passenger cars full of businessmen and visitors.

By the fall of 1903, the Cripple Creek–Victor Mining District had become a hotbed of labor unrest. Victor was the stronghold of the Western Federation of Miners, a powerful union that was making its influence felt in mining districts throughout the West. Miners and mill workers demanded an eight-hour workday, and when the owners refused, strikes were called. Violence wracked the district as mines were dynamited, thirteen non-union mine workers were killed when dynamite exploded at a railroad depot, and many more people were injured. Governor Peabody called in the National Guard and declared martial law, and hundreds of union sympathizers were arrested by "lawmen," who were really thugs hired by the mine owners. Two hundred union members were forced into railroad cars at gunpoint, hauled to the Colorado-Kansas border, dumped out, and ordered to never return. Gunshots were fired over the men's heads as they ran pell-mell into unknown territory, leaving their families behind in Victor.

This illegal deportation of union miners continued unchecked until the miners voted to end their strike in August 1904. Some mine owners never recovered financially from the strike and didn't resume mining operations. Working conditions didn't improve, and wages remained the same.

Around 1907, a young Victor miner named Jack Dempsey had aspirations of becoming a world-class boxer. He worked in the mines by day and trained in the gym above the Victor City Hall at night. One of his first fights was at the Gold Coin Club on Christmas night 1907. He defeated "Kid Blacky," starting his journey as the "Manassa Mauler," and eventually became the world's heavy-weight boxing champion in 1919.

The mine owners' troubles escalated when the deep tunnels began filling with water from underground streams. They built large, expensive tunnels, but this did not resolve the drainage problems. Mines began closing because this gold had become too expensive to mine. Work slowed, and miners and merchants abandoned the small satellite towns surrounding Cripple Creek and Victor.

In 1914, Richard Roelofs, a civil engineer with little mining experience, made the district's last great strike. He'd been working in the non-producing Cresson Mine for three years and had finally eked out $60,000 worth of gold ore. Then Roelofs discovered a "vug," which is a sparkling cave within the earth. This golden cave was actually a huge geode, and it was worth a fortune! The cavern was forty feet high, twenty-three feet long, and thirteen and a half feet wide, and it was full of gold. Its walls were covered by gold crystals and flakes that were nearly an inch wide. Roelofs installed a solid steel door in the tunnel entrance and hired three armed guards to protect his treasure. In just one week, his miners had scraped $378,000 worth of gold from the walls. Within one month, this cave produced $1.2 million worth of gold—that's over $20 million in today's dollars.

The Cresson bonanza gave the mining district a brief reprieve, but the exodus of miners continued. In 1936, the City of Victor, facing bankruptcy, raised $5,000 for its coffers by processing the waste soil in front of the post office. This material had come from the abandoned tailings of the rich Gold Coin Mine. They'd been dumped because the mine didn't bother processing any low-grade ore.

The Depression continued Victor's downward economic spiral, and World War II brought the federal government's mandate that mining could only be done to obtain "useful" minerals like copper, lead, and zinc for the war effort. Gold wasn't to be mined. Most Victor mines were shut down, and houses were boarded up as people left. The few who remained behind spent their days sitting around on street benches or crowding around potbellied stoves reminiscing about "Victor's good old days."

Tourists began to drift through town during the 1950s, and some, attracted by Victor's tumble-down buildings and forlorn appearance, stayed to paint pictures of the vacant streets, skeletal head-frames, and abandoned mines. In 1958, the Victor Museum opened, and in 1980, it was renamed the Lowell Thomas Museum, after one of the town's illustrious citizens. Lowell Thomas's father was a doctor who once had an office in the Victor Hotel. Lowell got his start delivering papers to Victor's saloons and brothels and went on to become a famous journalist and radio and TV broadcaster. Lowell Thomas was awarded the Medal of Freedom by President Ford in 1976. He traveled the world, and memorabilia from Thomas's long, illustrious career can be seen at the museum in the old office of the *Victor Record*.

Victor has about three hundred year-round residents now, and the Victor Downtown Historic District includes fifty-five of its sixty-six buildings. Many of these Neo-classical buildings are listed in the National Register of Historic Places, and Victor is a National Historic District.

In 1962, the Ajax Mine, which outlived all the others, stopped its operations after producing over $20 million in gold. Everyone thought this was the end of mining in the district, but when the price of gold began to go up in the

The San Juan Mountains are dotted with abandoned camps, old mines, and mining equipment. *Courtesy of Tom Williams.*

1980s, major mining companies became interested in Victor once again. Today, the Cripple Creek and Victor Gold Mining Company operates an open pit and leaching mine at the Cresson Mine, the largest in Colorado. It produces gold every year. The Cripple Creek–Victor Mining District has mined more gold than the California and Alaska gold rushes combined, and there's still a lot more, deep within the mountains.

Victor Hotel

Frank and Harry Woods struck it rich right away. They'd made money selling land, and now they were going to build Victor's first hotel. They had just started excavating the foundation when they struck gold, a twenty-inch-wide vein of the glittering stuff. They started mining immediately, and within a short time, the tall head-frame of their Gold Coin Mine dominated Main Street.

The brothers found another site for Victor's first hotel and built a three-story frame building that opened in July 1894. Five years later, it burned to the ground in the August 1899 fire, which caused $1.5 million in damages. The Woods Investment Company had become Victor's largest property owner and suffered the heaviest losses, including the total destruction of the bank and hotel. Frank and Harry shrugged off their losses because their Gold Coin Mine was bringing in as much as $50,000 a month.

They began building a new hotel, a four-story brick structure that took up most of a block on Victor Avenue. The Woods's First National Bank of Victor was on the ground floor, and a birdcage elevator carried lawyers, engineers, and businessmen to their offices on the second and third floors. Hotel rooms on the fourth floor rented for $2.50 per day, with a bath down the hall. The hotel's grand opening was on Christmas Eve 1899, and crowds gathered to admire the fancy Victorian wallpaper, fine furnishings, and pressed-metal ceilings.

The Victor Hotel is a Colorado Landmark Hotel and is included in the National Register of Historic Places. *Courtesy of Tom Williams.*

The Woods brothers had become immensely wealthy, and they had extensive real estate holdings, with assets of over $40 million, but their luck was changed by the 1899 fire. They lost many properties, and profits from the Gold Coin Mine, which had produced over $6 million, began to decline. Rumors of their financial troubles caused a run on their bank, and creditors circled as they tried to consolidate their holdings. Bank auditors declared their First National Bank insolvent and closed its doors. A grocery and jewelry store took over the first floor, and in 1904 A.E. Carlton, a wealthy mine owner, bought the entire Cripple Creek Mining District, plus the Victor Hotel. He established the City Bank on its first floor, retained the offices on the second and third floors, and converted the fourth floor into a hospital. In 1917, Carlton sold the bank to R.J. Gardner, who changed the bank's name to the Citizen's Bank of Victor. It operated briefly and was forced to close during the Depression. During this period, the small hospital was also closed, and the patients were moved to the St. Nicholas Hospital in Cripple Creek.

After the Woods brothers' financial empire collapsed, Harry moved to California and lived modestly until his death in 1928. Frank's son was killed in a mining accident in Colorado, and then both his wife and daughter died. He eventually remarried, but his second wife died, too. Frank tried several new business ventures, all of which failed. He moved to California, and when he died in 1932, his friends had to take up a collection for his burial.

The hotel building changed hands several times, and a variety of enterprises leased space there. A gift shop, restaurant, and soda fountain did business on the building's first floor during the 1950s, but the entire building was closed in the late 1960s. For the next twenty years, the Victor Hotel building sat vacant and deteriorating. In 1991, it was purchased in by the Victor Hotel Limited Liability Company.

After a $1 million renovation, the Victor Hotel reopened with its original bank vault and birdcage elevator in the Victorian lobby. Many historic elements of the old building were maintained but were updated to meet current building codes. The steam radiators were refurbished and fitted with individual thermostats in the rooms, while the ornate woodwork was refinished. The twelve-foot-high plate-glass windows, which are more than a century old, are still intact, and the original pressed-metal ceilings were cleaned and polished until they gleamed. Private baths were installed in the twenty guest rooms. The hotel, which looks much as it did in 1899, was placed on the National Register of Historic Places in 1980, and it is a Colorado Landmark Hotel.

The City Bank was located on the first floor of the Victor Hotel. *Courtesy of Tom Williams.*

GHOSTS

Many colorful characters have made the Victor Hotel their headquarters, and the old safe in the lobby once held millions of dollars in gold and currency. The Woods brothers made many huge investments, and high-powered mining executives and wealthy financiers often structured deals in their office. Now shadows of the hotel's glittering past linger in the halls, while restless spirits slip about, casting mysterious spells and whispering secrets. Guests have seen misty shapes and heard footsteps and laughter when no one's around. Sudden cold drafts, unexplained voices, and noises occasionally disturb the twilight hours.

The antique birdcage elevator still runs up and down between floors, taking guests to their rooms, and sometimes its passengers can't even be seen. Eddie McDermott worked in the mines in the early 1900s and boarded in room 301. He left for work every morning around 3:00 a.m., always taking the elevator to the lobby. One morning, Eddie pushed the button and called the elevator to the third floor. The doors opened, Eddie stepped in—and fell to his death, tumbling down the elevator shaft. There was no explanation for the tragedy, and Eddie's friends gathered in his room to mourn and toast his memory.

Guests in room 301 sometimes hear heavy footsteps in the hall stop outside their door, but there's never anyone there. Employees and guests have seen an older man in a flannel shirt and hat standing near room 301 or fiddling around with the elevator buttons.

A former hotel manager said a geology professor who stayed in room 301 for several days complained that he was often awakened by loud tapping noises coming from the radiator. One night, he awoke to see an older man tapping on the steam radiator, and then he slowly disappeared.

Guests in room 307 often complain that someone is banging on the pipes and that this clanking racket keeps them awake. There are no pipes in the walls that are near this room, and the noise can't be explained.

The apparition of an attractive young woman has been seen around the hotel by guests and employees. During the 2003 holiday season, she often passed through the lobby, stopping to admire the festive decorations, and then she simply vanished.

During the years when the fourth floor served as a hospital, injured miners were treated here. Some survived— some didn't. In the winter, when the ground was frozen, the bodies of the dead were kept in the hospital's morgue until the ground thawed enough in the spring for their burial. Many employees have reported seeing apparitions drifting through the fourth-floor halls, and voices have been heard when no one is around. Some shadowy forms seem to be missing an arm or a leg.

The Victor Hotel has been investigated by Mountain Peak Paranormal Investigations, Graves Paranormal Investigations and Research, and Colorado Paranormal Investigations. When Rocky Mountain Paranormal Investigations spent the night at the hotel, one member of the group made a recording of a hoarse voice that whispered, "Who are you?" Another investigator who stayed in 301, Eddie's room, heard a similar voice.

A couple from the Netherlands complained that they couldn't sleep in their room, 301, "because there was so much electricity in it." The lights and TV kept flickering on and off, and they were awakened by the sound of footsteps near the bed. When the light was flicked on, no one was there. The couple asked to be moved, but there were no other vacant rooms available. Determined to make the best of their situation, they tried to get some sleep again. The man had just managed to drift off when he awakened suddenly to see a misty figure standing at the foot of the bed. As he watched, terrified, the image slowly faded away. The remainder of the night, the couple was just too anxious to sleep, and they spent some more restless hours listening to the old elevator rattle up and down.

BIBLIOGRAPHY

Abbot, Carl, Stephen Leonard and David McComb. *Colorado: A History of the Centennial State*. Niwot: University Press of Colorado, 1994.
Abbot, Fay. *Beyond the Great Divide*. Ouray, CO: Western Reflections Publishing, 1999.
Aspinall, Richard. *Early History of Crested Butte*. Oakland, CA: Masalai Press, 1960.
Athearn, Robert. *The Denver and Rio Grande Western*. Omaha: University of Nebraska Press, 1977.
Bellanger, Jeff. *The World's Most Haunted Places*. Plimpton Place, NJ: New Page Books, 2011.'
Benham, Jack. *Silverton*. Ouray, CO: Bear Creek Publishing, 1981.
Brockett, D.A. *Wicked Western Slope*. Charleston, SC: The History Press, 2012.
Buys, Christian. *Historic Telluride in Rare Photographs*. Lake City, CO: Western Reflections, 1999.
Clarke, Alexandra. *Colorado's Historic Hotels*. Charleston, SC: The History Press, 2011.
Crofutt, George. *Grip-sack Guide to Colorado*. Boulder, CO: Johnson Books, 1985.
Crum, Josie. *The Rio Grande Southern Railroad*. Ouray, CO: San Juan History Inc., 1961.
Dallas, Sandra. *No More than Five in a Bed*. Norman: University of Oklahoma Press, 1967.
Davant, Jeanne. *Wellsprings: A History of the Pike's Peak Region*. Colorado Springs, CO: Gazette Enterprises, 2001.

Bibliography

Dody, Marilou. *Haunted Places in the Shadows of Pike's Peak*. Colorado Springs, CO: self-published, 2001.

Feitz, Leland. *A Quick History of Creede*. Colorado Springs, CO: Little London Press, 1969.

———. *A Quick History of Cripple Creek*. Colorado Springs, CO: Little London Press, 1983.

———. *A Quick History of Victor*. Colorado Springs, CO: Little London Press. 1969.

Haffen, LeRoy, and Ann Haffen. *The Colorado Story*. Denver, CO: Old West Publishing, 1960.

Harrison, Deborah. *The Cliff House*. Manitou Springs, CO: Historic Manitou Springs Publishing, 2007.

Henn, Roger. *Lies, Legends, and Lore of the San Juans*. Ouray, CO: Western Reflections Publishing, 1999.

Hull, Christine. *Cobwebs and Crystal: Colorado's Grand Old Hotels*. Boulder, CO: Pruett Publishing, 1982.

Huston, Richard. *A Silver Camp Called Creede*. Montrose, CO: Western Reflections Publishing, 2005.

Jarvis, Marian. *The Strater Hotel Story*. Durango, CO: Herald Publishing. 1969.

Kanla, Alan. *Grand Junction*. Charleston, SC: Arcadia Publishing, 2010.

Langdon, Emma. *Cripple Creek Strike*. New York: Arno Press, 1969.

Lavender, David. *The Rockies*. New York: Harper & Row, 1968.

Lell, Mabel. *Back in Cripple Creek*. Garden City, NY: Doubleday, 1968.

MacKell, Jan. *Cripple Creek District: The Last of Colorado's Gold Booms*. Charleston, SC: Arcadia Publishing, 2003.

McKee, Kathy, and Claudia Sutliff. *North Fork Valley*. Charleston, SC. Arcadia Publishing, 2012

McLean, Evalyn W. *Father Struck It Rich*. Lake City, CO: Western Reflections, 1999.

Munsell, Darrell. *From Redstone to Ludlow*. Boulder: University Press of Colorado, 2009.

Ninneman, John, and Duane Smith. *San Juan Bonanza*. Albuquerque: University of New Mexico Publishing, 2006.

Nossaman, Allen. *Many More Mountains*, Vols. 1–3. Denver, CO: Sundance Books, 1989.

Olsen, Mary. *The Silverton Story*. Cortez, CO. Beaber Printing Company, 1962.

Ragsdale, Terri. *A Legend of Grand Mesa*. Grand Junction, CO: Dreamtime Press, 2010.

Bibliography

Rust, Mary. *Historic Hotels of the Rocky Mountains*. Niwot, CO: Roberts Rinehart Publishing, 1997.

Sibley, George. *Crested Butte Primer*. Crested Butte, CO: Crested Butte Historical Society, 1972.

Sloan, Robert, and Carl Skrowrorski. *The Rainbow Route*. Denver, CO: Sundance Publishing, 2006.

Smith, Duane. *Crested Butte, from Coal Camp to Ski Town*. Lake City, CO: Western Reflections Publishing, 2006.

———. *Durango, Rocky Mountain Boom Town*. Boulder, CO: Pruett Publishing, 1986.

———. *The Irrepressible David F. Day*. Lake City, CO: Western Reflections, 2010.

———. *San Juan Legacy*. Albuquerque: University of New Mexico Publishing, 2009.

———. *The Song of the Hammer and Drill*. Boulder: University of Colorado Press, 2000.

Smith, P. David. *The Road that Silver Built*. Lake City, CO: Western Reflections, 2002.

Sprague, Marshall. *Money Mountain*. Boston: Little, Brown, 1953.

Stokes, Gerald. *A Walk Through Trinidad, CO*. Trinidad, CO: Trinidad Historical Society, 1986.

Tucker, T.F. *Otto Mears and the San Juans*. Montrose, CO: Western Reflections Publishing, 2003.

Twitty, Eric. *Basins of Silver*. Lake City, CO: Western Reflections Publishing, 2008.

Ubeloe, Carl, Maxine Benson, and Duane Smith. *A Colorado History*. Boulder, CO: Pruett Publishing, 2002.

Waters, Stephanie. *Ghosts of Colorado Springs and Pike's Peak*. Charleston, SC: The History Press, 2012.

———. *Haunted Manitou Springs*. Charleston, SC: The History Press, 2013.

Westerberg, Ann. *Colorado Ghost Tours: Haunted History and Encounters with the Afterlife*. Boulder, CO: Johnson Books, 2013.

Wiatrowski, Claude. *Railroads of Colorado*. St. Paul, MN: Voyageur Press, 2002.

Wildfang, Frederick. *Durango*. Charleston, SC: The History Press, 2009.

Wirth, Kelsey. *Reflections on a Western Town*. Crested Butte, CO: Oh, Be Joyful Press, 1996.

Wommack, Linda. *Colorado's Landmark Hotels*. Palmer Lake, CO: Filter Press, 2005.

BIBLIOGRAPHY

Wood, Richard. *Here Lies Colorado*. Helena, MT: Far Country Press, 2002.
Wyckoff, William. *Creating Colorado, The Making of a Western Landscape*. New Haven, CT: Yale University Press, 1999.
Wyman, Louis. *Snowflakes and Quartz*. Ouray, CO: Simpler Way Book Company, 1997.

About the Author

Exploring the mountains, the old abandoned mining camps and deserted diggings has always fascinated Nancy. A lifetime in the West has given her plenty of opportunities to learn about the many different people who struggled to carve out their lives amid its beauty and massive challenges.

Visit us at
www.historypress.com

www.ingramcontent.com/pod-product-compliance
Lightning Source LLC
Chambersburg PA
CBHW042142160426
43201CB00022B/2375